Praise for
THE CORE OF LEADERSHIP

"Jim Trunick's stories of winning from the middle are heartwarming, heart wrenching (punch here) and heart stretching. Having known Jim for over 10 years, he has been winning from the middle with a core of steel, an eternal smile and "how can I help you" presence. *The Core of Leadership* is one of those books that makes you laugh, cry and never put it down. Don't miss the Introduction with General Booth's quote on page 29. Thanks for sharing."

Betsy Allen, *CEO, MBA, CSP, MOK, Gaining Results, Inc.*

"Jim Trunick has been a 'leader of leaders' for the many years I have known him. His new book, which is strongly grounded in experience, is a powerful repository of wisdom, insight and truth valuable to all of us. *The Core of Leadership* will challenge your thinking, empower your will and refresh your spirit. Simply Excellent!"

Dr. Mike Dunphy, *Division Chair Sciences, Walsh University and Professional Speaker and Facilitator*

"Timeless (and quick!) reminders of what is at the core of being a leader, told with a passion that comes from experiencing great loss and success."

Verne Harnish, *Author of* Mastering the Rockefeller Habits

"In this engaging new book, Jim Trunick becomes your personal leadership coach as you explore what it takes to truly be a leader, not just at work, but also in your family and community. It's a book I highly recommend."

Kevin Kruse, New York Times *bestselling author,* We: How to Improve Performance and Profits Through Full Engagement

"A life journey in words, easy to relate to illustrations and practical tips on being a better leader in the workplace and a better person overall. Mr. Trunick has given the reader a look into what it takes to turn a manager into a leader and at the same time remind us what can happen when we focus on what is truly important."

Ron Lambert, *Past Chairman and Founder, Yukon Group Inc. and Author*

"Jim Trunick's book, *The Core of Leadership,* is filled with heartwarming stories and keen insights that enriched my appreciation for character, trust, family values, authenticity and humility. But what about Mr. Trunick's concept of leadership? His is not the 'I lead and you follow' model. Leadership is all about sticking to one's core values, transparency, learning and caring for others, whether they are your employees, partners, clients, spouse or children—not about demonstrating superior intelligence or skills. This easy read will make you look in the mirror and re-examine your own performance as a leader in all aspects of your life. I recommend it highly, whether or not you see yourself as an accomplished leader."

Tom Phelps, *Co-Founder Manatt, Phelps and Phillips, and board member CSUF Center of Leadership*

"I simply love this book, *The Core of Leadership*! Jim Trunick successfully undresses the false pretenses that often clouds people's perceptions and shows us the inner beauty of what it means to be an authentic leader. With compelling stories and insights, he masterfully breaks it all down into the pure essence of what it takes to effectively lead people and teams to success. Buy this book for your whole team and watch the results roll in. I give this book my highest recommendation!"

Tom Schulte, *Executive Director of Linked 2 Leadership and CEO of Recalibrate Professional Development*

"As someone who reads more than 100 business books a year and has studied leadership for nearly 20 years, I have a VERY high standard before I will endorse a book. I have just finished reading Jim Trunick's *The Core of Leadership* and I was incredibly impressed, touched and delighted. This is an absolutely wonderful book filled with superb stories, helpful advice and real leadership lessons. If you want to become a better leader and person—read this book!"

John Spence, *One of the Top 100 Business Thought Leaders in America*

"Over the course of my career I have spoken to over 3,000 corporations and business schools. I've seen leaders in all sizes, shapes, attitudes, and types. But I have never met anyone who exemplified the concepts Jim Trunick has brought forward in this work. Leading from the middle is exactly what companies should hope from their employees in the future. We live in a time where there is a premium placed on loyalty. Leading from the middle will increase the overall productivity of a company along with stimulating commitment from its people. Jim Trunick is an innovative voice and should be listened to by all of us who read this book."

Tom Sullivan, *Producer, Entertainer, Author, Lecturer,*
Advocate for Persons with Disabilities

"Jim is making a difference with his book, *The Core of Leadership*. What a refreshing and real way to look at leadership as Winning from the middle! We all want to be winners and leaders of our values, and Jim delivers thought-provoking insights, proven tactics and stories of how to actually make vulnerable, powerful. His passion for learning and truly insightful perspectives are a testament to his commitment to helping others grow. *The Core of Leadership* defines winning in a new way!"

Roz Usheroff, *President, The Usheroff Institute, Inc.,*
Author, Presenter and Executive Coach

The CORE of LEADERSHIP

The *CORE* *of* LEADERSHIP

Stories of
WINNING FROM THE MIDDLE

JIM TRUNICK

Advantage®

Published by Advantage, Charleston, South Carolina.
Member of Advantage Media Group.

ADVANTAGE is a registered trademark and the Advantage colophon is a trademark of Advantage Media Group, Inc.

Printed in the United States of America.

ISBN: 978-1-59932-374-9
LCCN: 2013946968

This publication is designed to provide accurate and authoritative information in regard to the subject matter covered. It is sold with the understanding that the publisher is not engaged in rendering legal, accounting, or other professional services. If legal advice or other expert assistance is required, the services of a competent professional person should be sought.

The information contained herein is provided in good faith, and every reasonable effort has been made to ensure that it is accurate and up to date.

In no event shall TrunickALC (LLC) be liable for any damage arising, directly or indirectly, from the use of this information. Including damages arising from inaccuracies, omissions or errors.

Advantage Media Group is proud to be a part of the Tree Neutral® program. Tree Neutral offsets the number of trees consumed in the production and printing of this book by taking proactive steps such as planting trees in direct proportion to the number of trees used to print books. To learn more about Tree Neutral, please visit www.treeneutral.com. To learn more about Advantage's commitment to being a responsible steward of the environment, please visit www.advantagefamily.com/green

Advantage Media Group is a publisher of business, self-improvement, and professional development books and online learning. We help entrepreneurs, business leaders, and professionals share their Stories, Passion, and Knowledge to help others Learn & Grow. Do you have a manuscript or book idea that you would like us to consider for publishing? Please visit advantagefamily.com or call 1.866.775.1696.

To my wife, Cindy, guiding me through grace.

ACKNOWLEDGEMENTS

Tom Sullivan Tom and his wife Patty impact and inspire so many people. Tom is a mentor, sponsor and friend. Having gone through his life blind since birth, never seeing Patty's face or a sunset, is not sad—rather a journey most of us don't face. His other senses are heightened to levels most of us never touch. Through the books he has written, the songs he's composed, attending Harvard, and donating vast amounts of time and money to the Blind Children's Center, he lives courageously. Building hope in himself that from being a very scared little boy—he will be loved. He is loved by so many and a public voice who inspired this book. Great guy—and don't ever say to him, "here are the keys—you drive." He might actually try! Thanks Tom.

Advantage Media Group team. Thanks to Brooke, Megan, Alison, Kim, Bob, Denis, Adam, George, Amy, Patti, and Jenn, for your guidance, insight and expertise, to help me turn years of journaling into a book; a real book. You helped me and others find our way, less to the top of organizations of success, but rather to the center of values and heart, to be more significant. Thank you, Verne, for guiding me to this outstanding Advantage team.

My Family. Cindy and our kids, are not public. They have become more centerpieces to winning from the middle, more transparent and exposed than they ever intended. They push themselves outside their comfort zone, to support me, in my desire to share leadership values. I am so grateful to them, and appreciate greatly their finding their core of leadership, as I am learning about mine.

Love,

Jim

Jim can be reached at **Trunickalc@aol.com**
Author photo by Photo Boutique

ABOUT THE AUTHOR

J im Trunick is currently a senior director of commercial leadership development with a major health-care company. In this
role he oversees sales coaching and marketing management
as well as leadership development. He is a certified instructor with
Maximum Impact, DDI, Blanchard Management, Human Performance Institute (Corporate Athlete; Power of Full Engagement),
Discovery Insights Behavior Development, Yukon Negotiations
Master trainer and Covey's 7 Habits.

He has more than 25 years of health-care industry experience
including pharmaceutical sales and sales management, product
marketing, professional relations, and U.S. sales operations.

Mr. Trunick is on the board of directors and a vice president of
the Society of Pharmaceutical and Biotech Trainers.

"I am more the student, less the expert," he says, explaining that his early interest in veterinary school evolved into
a career in sales and leadership development. "Professional
selling," he says, "is about creating buyers, not pushing

product. Nobody comes home from a shopping trip with packages, saying, 'Hey, look what somebody sold me!' They say, 'Look what I bought!' Leadership is similar. We think of great leaders as people of supreme confidence, oration skill, or courage. I believe it is simpler than that: It's about upholding beliefs and values over rewards."

TABLE OF CONTENTS

LIVING, LOVING, LEARNING

S uch a tender age to be defining life as a struggle. Megan is only eight, and she is dealing with thoughts and nightmares that no one, particularly a child, should confront. Her mother was her world.

It's 1999, and the year has not been kind to Megan. She cannot grasp what is happening to her mother, who is nearing the end of her life. Until now, Megan danced through her days, like a typical third-grader. Now, she tries to be normal, and she feels very much onstage. "Why are you so mad all the time?" her little friends ask her, or "Why are you being so silly?"

Several days before Teri's passing, all three of our children and I head out to visit her at City of Hope hospital. In her Sunday skirt,

Megan climbs into the car for the family journey to church and then to the hospital, an hour away. As she wrestles with her brothers in the car, I get upset.

Getting dressed this day has been ordeal for both Megan and me. I couldn't find a clean shirt, and Megan wanted me to iron her skirt. "You can iron silk, right?" she asked. And as she watched, I touched the too-hot iron to her favorite purple skirt, destroying it.

Now, already late for church, I speed through the rain and pull into a Starbucks, parking haphazardly. I slam the car door, telling kids to stay where they are and not destroy anything.

"So where are you heading?" asks a woman in line with me.

"Church!" I bark.

"Well, by the way you were driving, I don't want to be part of that church!"

About noon, we arrive at the hospital. We are preparing to have Teri come home, unaware of her infections. She is moving more slowly than just two days ago and struggles to get into her wheelchair. She feels chilly, but she still wants to go out to the hospital garden to watch our children play.

I sit on a cold concrete bench next to Teri in her wheelchair. We sit quietly, watching Jeff chasing Brian and Megan around the garden maze. "Aren't they beautiful?" Teri says.

It's a moment I know I will never forget. She has lost her hair, her face is puffy, and her body is weak from all the steroids and cyclosporine therapy of post bone-marrow transplant for her CML leukemia. And we are together, smiling at our children.

Eight days later, Teri dies.

At the funeral, Brian, age 12, puts his arm around Megan. They are struggling to understand. Mom's gone, and she's in that box now? Everyone's crying, and they've done their share of that too, for many weeks. As the middle child, Brian is Mr. Harmony, doing whatever he can for others to keep himself busy and stay in their favor.

Teri's long illness has left Brian shaken, quiet, introspective, and depressed. His pain is obvious, and his ability to communicate his feelings is weak. I have been talking with him every day, to little avail.

"My friends say I didn't love Mom very much if I'm not crying all the time," he finally says to me one day. "I guess I didn't pray so good."

I'm at a loss for words. "I get teased at school," he continues, "for being quiet." He has even encountered cruelty. "I'm going to tell your mom," one boy yelled at him over some childish nonsense. "Oh, wait, that's right! You don't have one!"

As far as I can remember, all the kids I knew when I was growing up had two parents. And now, here I am raising three kids without their mom. Some of what I was encountering was outside my training as a parent, and really, what had been the training?

I look at Brian. Whatever lessons I'm learning in my career, I tell myself, pale in comparison to the hard lessons this little one is learning about life right now.

At 15, my other son, Jeff, is harboring his own troubles as he deals with Teri's death. He doesn't seem to care anymore about anything. Friends have begun to offer him alcohol and drugs, and his response, I learn, has been "Sure." Hard lessons come in many forms.

Sometimes curling up into a ball seems to be the best option.

LEADERSHIP TEMPERATURE CHECK

It seems to me the crucibles, or severe tests and trials, in our lives, shape our success and leadership. The term crucible refers to the application of heat melting one substance into creating another. The crucibles of our lives shape our daily, living leadership. I recall the phrase, "calm seas raise amateur sailors!" Life lessons aren't reserved for an asterisk or footnote to leadership results—they are the real deal.

I was asked several years ago to give a talk on coaching and sales leadership. And as I began to put my thoughts together, I wondered, what did I have to really say about leadership? My lessons were not special, and so I labored through my notes, trying to make sense of the message I wanted to convey. As I thought about others, and my struggle becoming a single parent, and raising kids as a mom and dad, and realizing how inadequate I was, I found my voice. My leadership was and is a product of my life lessons. My struggles to learn and grow have shaped my thinking for others and the basis of that presentation and this book.

"Hello?" Megan says, answering the phone. It's several months after her mom's death and she and I are making sandwiches for her summer camp.

"No," she says into the receiver, "not here." There's a pause. "Heaven." Pause, "okay?" she says, and hangs up. She continues making her sandwich and says to me, "Daddy, next time the phone rings, will you get it?" My heart sank.

"Sure, Megan," I said, impressed by her composure and matter-of-fact maturity. I saw how she was dealing with loss.

As I look back, I realize it was at that point that my sense of parenting and understanding of leadership took a new turn that would shape my relations with family, friends, neighbors, and colleagues.

Pain is inevitable, I realized. Misery is an option. I have learned through pain that if you choose misery, it hurts you more than anyone else. Pain shapes our world, and it can either harden the heart or soften it.

One day I returned a call from a neighbor. For quite some time, she told me, she had been putting daily notes in her son's lunchbox, sometimes a comforting word of scripture, sometimes just "I love you." Her son was adopted, and she was trying to help him see how much he was loved.

"I thought you'd like to know something," she told me. "Until recently, I always found those notes still in his lunchbox after school each day. But then they were missing. I thought at first he'd started throwing them away." She said her son explained that he'd been giving them to a boy at school who seemed to need them more than he did. The boy's mother had been very sick with leukemia.

"I know it's your Brian who has been getting those notes," the neighbor told me, "and I want you to know we're concerned about you and your family."

Later I asked Brian about it, and he sheepishly gave me the collection of notes, thinking he might be in trouble. I put my arms around him and cried. "You can keep all those notes," I told him.

I could see that the notes meant everything to him. Brian's pain was quiet. He didn't talked about his mother, and many of his friends weren't nearly as patient with him as I would have liked.

To me, those notes symbolize that we all have one degree of separation from cancer. There is always cause to care, and those were indeed notes of caring: love, praise, hope, and joy. It is our humanity that is first and foremost. Whether you are dealing with family, neighbors or coworkers, if you want good results, you must be in touch with humanity.

Everyone has stories of pain and hardship, and these are not to be paraded about. However, to the extent that it is appropriate, I have learned that sharing and transparency are healing and powerful.

In my career, I give many presentations and speeches, and several years ago I began to consider sharing my family's story with total strangers. Transparency is a cornerstone to building trust. I can't think of a more relevant and powerful way to build it. Yes, it's risky, and isn't that also what makes trust so special? It's earned, not expected.

Let me say this: Teri was my college sweetheart. She liked my laugh when she heard it across the room at a party. I liked her smile and how I felt being around her. I was two years older, and after I graduated, we dated for two years. I worked in sales, and she finished up her degree in psychology at Ohio State. We married in 1979, and Jeff was born in 1983, then Brian in 1987, and Megan in 1990.

We'd moved from Ohio to California. For Teri, who grew up in Chillicothe, Ohio, the move to California was difficult. Her parents were both teachers, and they didn't travel much, but we made California work.

In November 1994, Teri had a regular checkup, including a pap smear. Her doctor called her two days later while I was at work. "We've gotten your blood results back. A normal white cell count is about 5,000. Your count is 125,000. You have leukemia."

She was so stunned that she couldn't even call me. She told me six hours later as I walked through the door. What? How? No!

Over the next few years we looked for a donor match, including tests on family members. The closer the match, the better chance is for recovery from host-graft disease. And Teri had another concern: Megan was only three and couldn't read, and she didn't want surgery until Megan could read.

We faced the situation, and we endured. There's not much more to say about that.

My sense of responsibility and caring and pain left me with a big hole that I could not fill. Eventually I built an improved sense of self, and that came from taking care of my children. I trusted in my desire to be a better dad and mom. My goals changed, and my values shifted to family.

I recall not caring about work. Being a good employee seemed a low priority. I felt cranky, with a trigger temper. I waited for someone to give me a hard time about anything. I sharpened my tongue and aimed it at the poor soul crossing my path.

Teri wanted to be buried in Ohio. She had long missed her small rural town, where her parents were the math teacher and school librarian. It pleased her family that she could be buried near them, and it also would give me and the children a good reason to travel there to visit with them.

After her burial, I heard rumors at work that I would be moving back to Ohio, even though California was my home and where I worked. Although I had no such plans, the rumors mounted, as did the impression that, with all those hospital visits, I was not pulling my weight at work. My tongue was sharpened for the inevitable challenge.

I called a meeting with my boss to clarify my situation. Teri had passed away only three weeks earlier. I announced to my boss that I was back and prepared to pick up the slack. I was not moving to Ohio, I emphasized, and he could count on me. Back in uniform, and ready to report to duty, sir. Ship shape and ready to go. You can count on me. I'm your man ...

My boss sat across from me, a half smile on his face, and sadness in his eyes. "Jim, this place was here long before Teri got sick, and we have got mounds of work for you to do, and right now, you need to go home, be with your kids, and take care of them. We'll keep the lights on for you, and we are here when you are really ready and able to work. But now, your kids need you."

I held back the tears. I was being sent home, and it was exactly the right call. Over the next three weeks, I began to slowly emerge, with my tongue less sharp and my heart full of the sense of caring that I had been shown. Others had shown that they cared about me, even when I cared so little about myself.

MY STORY IS LIKE YOURS

I read once that to stumble is to move forward more quickly. Stumble I did—and do. My story is like yours, and through my experiences, I shape my view of the world and others. I know how important having friends and trustees is to being a better person. It saddens me that my son Brian seems to have few friends.

As I tackle this book, I go through old video clips and photographs, trying to make my writing an all-out expression of humanity—my humanity. I've learned that leadership is far more than generals on horseback with flashing swords. You find it in many places other than on brightly lighted podiums where men in suits expound upon their grand schemes. When did leadership become so elitist?

Leadership is daily, and it is living. Regular folks strive for it, trying to better our world. Sometimes we tell, sometimes we ask. We get it right and we get it wrong. John Wayne said our greatest gift is tomorrow. We can apply what we learned yesterday to begin a fresh tomorrow.

I'm not a CEO. I do not have a PhD, although I was a PHD (poor, hungry, determined) when I was hired. I am a trainer, a developer of people, a connector of sorts. I know the CEOs and janitors, and they know me. That's power, the kind of power that comes from leading in the middle. The middle is the core of organizations, and of society, and we must strengthen our core, just as we strengthen the core of our bodies through exercise and the martial arts.

If our core is strong, we can lead with strength. My own core strengthens as I reflect on my past, learning and projecting for a better outcome. We also learn from acknowledging our mistakes and weaknesses, for, in that, we are more human. Leadership, for me, is about knowing our humanity.

LEADERSHIP LEARNED FROM LIFE

Should leadership be taught as a profession in schools, the way lawyers and doctors are trained? Simply put: no. Doctors and lawyers have special knowledge, as do many professionals. Many people, however, will tell you that they value life's lessons more than the ones they learned in class. Some of the greatest lessons of leadership come from housewives and soccer moms, like Frances Hasselbein, Mary Kay, and Clara Barton. Real leadership arises from the heart. It is not licensed.

Leadership is a choice. You can choose to stay positive and in the moment, or you can let yourself be full of doubt and negativity. It takes as much energy to be frustrated as it does to be resourceful, and it's hard to be both at the same time.

If you ask the top performers on the job how they reach success, you often hear: "I don't know. I just do it." Ask a great athlete how he made that touchdown or how she made that shot, and you'll see that it's what comes naturally, with the help of good training. They have the right habits, and the best have a passion. Learning to do well is a matter of wanting to learn. We all know success is less about the name of the college you attended and more about what you do with the education and knowledge you have.

Years ago, on an episode of the television show *M*A*S*H*, the character Hawkeye needed a surgical procedure and had to decide which surgeon to use: his friend BJ Honeycutt or the world-renowned Major Winchester. Hawkeye chose BJ. As he explained to the deflated and angry Winchester, he chose his friend because if anything went wrong, his friend would try harder to make it better. Winchester, by contrast, would think he knew it all and nothing could go wrong.

As Hawkeye explained: "I want the team I surround myself with to break a sweat, determined to improve and grow, and be less about blaming situations on people or events in the past." We should all want that. You need a team around you that you are confident will deliver the very best.

Things go wrong, despite our best plans and efforts. What kind of leader will you be: the one pointing to the reason things went wrong, or the one in the mirror, determined to learn and fight harder to make things better? That's leadership, and it's your choice.

Tough times don't build character; they reveal it. If you're at a business conference and a taxi driver hands you two receipts, what do you do? Do you take both receipts and put them on your expense account? Or do you tell the cab driver, "No thank you. I just need the one"? Those little moments when we may wobble in our ethics speak volumes about us and our prospects for overall success.

Ernest Hemingway, in *The Sun Also Rises*, succinctly describes how a character went bankrupt: "Two ways. Gradually, then suddenly." Our lives, and our values, can play out that way as well. We eat doughnuts instead of apples, day by day, until our health disintegrates. Our daily missteps can lead to habits that shape our outcome. What we do in our daily lives needs to reflect our larger goals, or we will miss the mark.

At times, when watching college football, I'm reminded of a lesson in ethics. A player catches the ball near the ground and drops it, and everyone knows it, yet he stands up and holds the ball high as if to say, "Look at me. I caught it." The video shows the truth, and yet the player tries to claim otherwise. My son and I were watching football one Sunday, and when this actually happened during the game, he said, "Well, if you ain't cheating, you ain't trying." Well, that walked him into a long conversation he hadn't planned.

Are we so eager to look right that we fudge the truth, with our families or with our colleagues, to claim the catch that isn't ours? How much better to toss the ball back to the referee and say, "No, I didn't catch it"? That's the sense of ethics that we need in business and at home if we truly want success. That's the wellspring of leadership.

"Does the dream make the person, or the person make the dream?" asks John Maxwell, author of many books focusing on leadership. He concludes that it's both, each about half the time. If the dream is bigger than you, he said, you have only two options: you can quit, or get help. It's a long road to leadership, and we live it out daily. You need not travel alone.

THE ABCs OF
LEADERSHIP

T he founder of the Salvation Army, General William Booth, was too aged and ill to attend the fiftieth anniversary celebration in 1915. So he was asked to write a letter that would speak to the hearts of the delegates. He sent the following telegram: "Dear delegates: 'Others' (signed, General Booth)."

And that was all. Nothing more needed to be said. Of everything I have read about leadership, that one word encapsulates what it is all about. In fact, if I were told that I must condense this book to a single word, that one very well might be the word I would choose.

We need others, in so many ways. The dynamics of leadership cannot readily be defined as those who are in charge and those who follow. Our best leaders were great followers first, and through history some our best followers have been our greatest leaders. Abraham Lincoln was a private in the army. Martin Luther King lived and breathed nonviolence and passive protest, and today he is revered as the epicenter of huge social change. Clara Barton was a nurse who went on to found the Red Cross. My mother was a daughter first!

Throughout history, society has at times sentenced its worst offenders to long periods of solitary confinement. Being without others can be the ultimate pain. We exist to be with others, and without them, we may die. Even when our relationships cause us distress, seldom do we go off to be hermits. We're not wired that way.

Rather, we are wired to participate in activities. And in those activities, the more we participate, the more we learn. In other words, we must actually "do." Sitting and listening can only get you so far. We absorb more when we put what we hear into practice, particularly when we work with others who hold us accountable. The following quote has been attributed to so many people that its truth must be self-evident: "To know and not to do is really not to know."

We are moving toward leadership when we begin to teach others through our example and actions. The most defining measure of a failure of leadership is when we know what we must do and yet fail to do it. Doing what is right requires energy.

There is an old story about three frogs on a big leaf floating down the river. One of the frogs decides to jump off the leaf into the water. How many frogs are left on the leaf? The answer is three. Just because that frog decided to jump doesn't mean that he did. Willpower alone is not enough; we must apply ourselves. We can know we should lose weight, for example, and decide that's what we will do. We may know just what we need to do to lose weight. But unless we take the steps to do it, we accomplish nothing.

When the deciding and the doing are in alignment, we are making progress—in business, at home, and in our sense of ourselves.

WHY I AM WRITING THIS BOOK

When I began to put down the words for this book, I was searching for an outlet for the life lessons that experience had taught me and was teaching me. In a way, it was a therapy for me. As I have shared these perspectives with other business leaders, this book has evolved, over the course of several years, into one on how to manage and lead.

Yes, there is much here that can be applied in a corporate setting. But I believe the lessons here are for mothers and fathers, sisters and brothers, bosses and employees, and all those who feel others don't understand them. Think about it: don't almost all of our anxieties and fears stem from others not knowing us or wanting to know us? When you hear anyone say that he or she doesn't care what others think, know this: it's not true. We do care.

In this book, I will share numerous stories and insights that I hope will make you more transparent, quick to listen, and slow to speak. If you want to learn from the heart, this book is for you. It's the heart, not the head, that is the center of leadership, and it must embrace others, as General Booth knew so well.

My good friend Ed told me about an experience he had as he and a friend headed to a golf outing near San Diego and passed the Miramar Air Force Base next to the freeway. As a jet fighter approached for a landing, its tires nearly touched the runway, and then the engines roared and turned fiery red as the jet zoomed skyward.

"Whoa!" Ed said. "What's going on there?"

His friend glanced at the runway. "Oh, they're just doing touch-and-go's." He explained that the pilots were practicing the difficult art of landing on an aircraft carrier. They needed to practice. They must be prepared.

I hope the stories in this book will touch you and inspire you to get going with life—and yes, life can be full of difficult landings and can challenge us to quick take-offs. I hope to inspire better parents, workers, leaders, teachers, and givers. I hope to move you to share your own stories. By living honestly, openly, and authentically, you will feel better, and that makes you more attractive to others.

That's leadership. I have a long way to go, I know. I will open my heart, and I hope that you will open your heart, too.

A TEAM MEMBER'S PROBLEM

Trey came to his review ready to be promoted. Well, that wasn't going to happen. As I went through his accomplishments and successes, he seemed quiet, and not overly excited. I thought he would really value the praise. After we reviewed his performance, and looked at goals for the next year, he seemed distant. Trey said, "So this means promotion to senior executive right? You haven't even mentioned that!" I clarified he had a good sales year, and was not in-line for advancement given his limited tenure, although his experience in showing leadership was beyond the day-to-day sales responsibilities. He was upset. He really pushed back, and seemed mad. He went off, and backed me up in a negative way. What I had already covered

THE ABCS OF LEADERSHIP

was being highlighted now as reasons for his promotion, not simply accolades for a job well done.

I thought this was going to be a good review with a top employee, and an easy session, versus other talks I was preparing with his team members, which I thought might be tough. As I listened, I really listened, though nobody likes to be surprised—I was blind-sided by his frustration and emotion. After his rant, I really paused, and seemed quiet. I finally said, after a moment of silence, "What's really eating you?" He continued with his expectation for promotion. I said, "No!" I never told you that, or indicated anything other than you need to continue growing in your current role. No, this is you. Why are you so adamant, and we've never had this conversation. What's really eating you?" After 10 more minutes, he finally broke down, and told me his wife was upset with his hours and he had told her that morning that he was going to get his promotion today! She was thrilled? Oh, well that's different. You are upset with me, as you committed to your wife a result I was not prepared to deliver. He cried. I was so taken aback and realized that one of my high performers was struggling.

Trey and I had a good talk, about his status with me, and our team. Then we talked about how to position his lack of promotion to others and family, who may be expecting that next step. We reviewed the what, how and goals, and mostly what to say and not say to people to be in-line with a clearer version of the truth he and I shared. We practiced what and how to say things to others. He left prepared to let others know he was tracking for promotion, and had more work to do, with specific timelines.

Trey, was promoted a year later, and then moved to management. He grew his career through admitting failure and doubt, and we worked together to shape the future he wanted. His learning went on to serve many people in many situations. He thanked me years later at an awards banquet for the management success of his team, for that how-to-tell-others meeting about his over-promotion of himself at home. And I just smiled, as his success was already my reward—I thanked him, for carrying on in the face of weakness (so many run) to other relationships or organizations, embarrassed. Not Trey: he learned. He grew, and many benefitted!

THE MEASURE OF A LEADER

It's an age-old question: how do you measure successful leadership? What is the return on investment? My nephew recently asked me that question as he was writing his thesis at Miami University. "Well," I said, "it is twofold and very simply comes down to this: 1) How do you feel Sunday night before you go to work Monday morning? and 2) what do you see when you look into the eyes of the person who is your most important relationship? Not favorite or worst relationship, most important."

We waste time and effort in trying to measure the return on investment (ROI) of something that involves people's emotions as if we were counting cars produced per hour. It's time to stop. The methods of yesteryear do not necessarily apply today. Go ahead and depend on time clocks and rigorous scheduling if you find it improves performance and loyalty. If you are running a team, however, you may be running out of time. In a society of new workers, there's a better way to enhance productivity and value, and it involves inspiration and motivation.

In *First, Break All the Rules*, author Marcus Buckingham points out that 55 percent of American workers don't care. Can you imagine being the chief executive officer of a company and finding out that 55 out of 100 workers to whom you pay salary, expenses, bonuses, and benefits don't care? You can try to manage them, scold them, lecture, and penalize them, and you can try any number of carrots and sticks, to little avail. Or you can listen, get on board, engage their values and attitudes—and find your company soaring.

So often, managers talk in terms of what they are doing for employees, and the employees talk in terms of what the managers are doing "to" them. Good leadership has the best ROI when it motivates through emotion and persuades through reason, and that return is in the eye of the beholder.

All business success starts with leadership. It can start with a quiet, pensive type of personal leadership that one exhibits when writing a poem or song, or analyzing a molecule. It requires leadership to shape ideas into products and services. We show leadership when we strive for personal goals, or when, as supervisors, we uphold organizational goals because we want to lead, not because we are paid to do so.

LEADERSHIP AS A JOURNEY

It has been called living leadership, and it is a journey, a personal and professional one. It is the journey of developing the leader within us, the leader whom we want to become and whom we want others to see. It is our life journey to significance.

Some people say, "I don't want to be a leader; that's not my calling. I'm just more interested in being a better me." Perhaps we are focused on making more money, having more fun, being a better spouse, friend, or contributor. Through it all, we become leaders simply through our daily actions. Success or failure results from our character.

Why write about it, then, if leadership is just life moving along as we do the best we can? What's new about that? The answer is simple: if we don't keep in touch with all our emotions, the world becomes less for each of us. In order for us to fully appreciate all that we are, or what life can be, we need to connect with our emotions.

Have you ever talked to someone who has gone through a difficult time, perhaps divorce, bankruptcy, death of a loved one? You notice that they go through phases of pain, anger, sadness, acceptance, and eventually, for many, joy. Ten people see a movie or hear a story, and some laugh, others frown, and yet others cry. Like movies, life hits us all differently. We strive to understand a complex world of people trying for success with unclear models and visions for what that even means. It's a different picture for each of us, and that's why we take this journey together. True leadership demands that we work with one another.

Recently, in a college softball championship, Sara Tucholsky, a Western Oregon University player, hit a three-run home run in the last inning to win 4–2. Yet, as she rounded first base, she hurt her ankle so badly that she could only crawl back to first base. According to the rules, she had to touch all the bases for her home run to count, without help from her teammates. If she stayed at first, her hit would only count as a single.

Two players on the opposing team, Mallory Holtman and Liz Wallace of Central Washington, asked the umpires whether the home run would be declared official if they helped her touch each base. Nothing in the rule book prevents the opposition from helping, the umpires said. So, in the spirit of true sportsmanship, they carried her to each base, and she gently touched each base with her good foot. Although Central Washington was thereby eliminated from the playoffs, those players answered to the higher calling of caring.

That's what daily leadership is all about. It's about a victory that goes beyond the box score. It's the kind of leadership that says, "If you want to go fast, go alone. If you want to go far, go together." You need a sense of helping one another.

THE UBUNTU PHILOSOPHY

Several years ago I had the opportunity to meet Doc Rivers, the famous basketball coach for the Boston Celtics, now LA Clippers, talk about putting that team together. In the years when the team wasn't winning, he said, everybody worked on the fundamentals and pitched in to take care of one another, doing the small things, even carrying the water buckets. After becoming champions, he said, people say, "I'm not carrying the water buckets. I'm a champion." Egos get in the way. Doc Rivers talked about the Ubuntu philosophy that maintains, "I am because we are," and that mantra continues to live on as an example of great leadership. The individual owes his or her achievement to the values of the group.

Winning should indeed be more than a box score. It's in the hearts of the players and in the character of the teams. A *Wall Street Journal* article asserted that business should have much in common with amateur athletics, in which the emphasis is on sportsmanship, fair play, and hard work. However, the article warned that business must never sacrifice its integrity, which can happen in professional sports with so much riding on each play.

There are a multitude of examples in the business world in which greed leads to actions that are like the performance-enhancing cheating that has tainted the reputations of some in the sports world. That's what can happen when individuals feel that they are in it for themselves. Were we all to embrace the Ubuntu philosophy, which says, in essence, "I am nothing without the team," we would fare much better in sports, in business, in life.

NOT EASY GROWING A TEAM

Regina accepted my job offer. I knew she would, as we had some good discussions in her interview about selling. She had not sold much before, but her character was beyond reproach. She put herself through school, including a full scholarship for tennis at UCLA. She had a high grade point and incredible references from coaches and competitors. Regina was bright and determined, and I was so glad to have her on board. She was an African American woman hired to work in a city with a customer base of primarily older white men. This was her first job out of college, and a risk for me, to hire someone without experience.

One of my senior salespeople, Pam, said she really liked Regina. About that time, rumors were flying about how Regina was too young and probably not going to make it. Pam, pulled me aside one day, and said, "Have you seen what Regina is wearing?" I said, "Yes, a professional tan suit." Pam said, "...and have you, in any of her interviews, ever seen her wear anything else?" I thought, and said, "Ah, come to think of it, no." Pam said, "Jim, her suit is a stained, torn mess." I listened, and Pam told me, "It is the only suit she owns. Regina is broke, and her family had to borrow from Goodwill to get the suit she is wearing every day." Pam went on. "Her hair and personal hygiene is not going to be suitable for calling on hospitals and surgeons, as she does not look professional, and accounts will not respect her."

Pam was always professionally dressed and well-received by her accounts. Pam agreed to help me, and took Regina shopping and to a salon the following Saturday. She came to work the following week. Unbelievable. The same character and integrity I hired, was now looking like a new showroom! My boss, who interviewed her earlier, asked me who she was, and I said "Regina." He said, "No, the gal in the blue suit?" I said, smiling, "Regina." He was stunned. Regina went on to be runner-up for the rookie of the year award, and a top performer. Regina was promoted four years later to district manager. She later got married, started a family and started her own business, and has 36 employees, working for her in a generic-medicine distribution company.

I learned to hire the things you can't train or fix. Suits and hair are more easily fixed than work ethic, integrity and character! Go Regina, and thanks to Pam!

LEADERSHIP IS NOT A COMPETITION

Leadership, for many people, looks like a competition. It's not. John Maxwell has said, "My success is achieved through others. My lessons are learned from others. My weaknesses are strengthened by others, my servanthood tested under others, my influence compounded through others, my best given to others, my legacy left for others."

Several years ago, an associate asked me to go for a run when we both were attending an out-of-town meeting. I ran track in college, but over the years my knees started to bother me. I hadn't run as much. He persisted, and I agreed to join him. We got up early one morning and began our run. Within a mile I couldn't keep pace with him. "Can we slow down?" I asked, and he did—for a while. Soon he was so far in front of me that I couldn't see him. I was lost in a strange town. I made my way back to the hotel, where I overheard my running partner talking to somebody in the hall: "Jim? Oh, I have no idea where he is. As far as I know, he's still out there running." His gesture of friendship seems to have been based solely on the competitive spirit.

A neighbor to whom I told that story related to me an experience of a far different nature. My neighbor had wanted to become a member of a bicycling team. When he went with the group on a Sunday ride, he trailed the others. One of his friends slowed down to chat, and after about 15 minutes pointed out, "Hey, looks like we've caught up!" His friend, without saying a word, had put a hand on my neighbor's bike seat and pedaled faster to help him catch up, knowing how much my neighbor wanted to be part of the group. His was a spirit of humility, and that, not competition, is what great leadership is all about.

CLOSER TO OUR POTENTIAL

There's a cost to leadership: sometimes we have to give up our own personal rights for the greater responsibility of the team. My boss, when I first started in business, told me, "It's an employee's right to complain." I think what he was saying was that as you move up into leadership, you have to be aware that you give up your right to complain and to whine and to blame other situations. You have a responsibility to listen, to be patient, to understand the needs of others, and to truly be responsible to a greater organizational calling. "For employees, it's a picnic; for you, it's a business meeting," said the Fortune Group's W. Steven Brown, author of *13 Fatal Errors Managers Make: And How You Can Avoid Them.* Leaders need to understand that they are always on stage.

Hundreds of studies on leadership have led to no clear results. In large part that is because we are dealing with people, with others, all with special gifts and talents. Some of those gifts and talents go unexpressed. The goal of leadership development is to gain the insights and perspectives that will get us closer to realizing our greatest potential.

Think of an iceberg, of which so much lies below the surface. Human behavior and attitudes are like that. What we see are our behaviors, and they are shaped by the environment. We see and hear them, and we measure the results in terms of competence and intellect. The bottom part of the iceberg—what's that? Well, that consists of the values, the attitudes, the feelings, the beliefs—the much bigger part of this metaphor for a human. In fact, that bigger part actually shapes the top part. Values, attitudes, and beliefs have more to do with success, at home and in business, than the top part, and yet all we tend to look at is the top part.

THE EVOLUTION OF LEADERSHIP

I remind myself, through these writings, of the things that I should be doing, and hopefully I am adding value for others. First we follow the leader, and second, we follow his/her vision. It starts with the person, and I am learning to be a better one.

I had the chance several years ago to meet Dick Enberg, the famous broadcaster. As he shared stories of athletes he'd met, I heard leadership messages woven into his stories. When asked who his favorite athlete was, he said with barely a pause, "Johnny Bench." The Hall of Fame baseball catcher of *my* Cincinnati Reds!

Why Johnny Bench, among the many celebrities he could have named? Dick grew up in a household where basketball ruled, he said. His dad was a very successful high-school basketball coach, and Dick was dedicated to building himself into one of his dad's best players. However, despite the "inside help" from his dad, Dick never rose to greatness as a player. Playing basketball for his dad was not going to be a reality.

Still, Dick loved basketball, and after working at a local radio station as a janitor, he got a chance to read some sports news, and even practice announcing a few high-school games. As Dick applied his learning of hard work and discipline to his craft, he excelled and became the "voice of the Bruins" during the John Wooden UCLA Bruin basketball excellence in the 1960s. Always just a phone call away from his dad, he won the Emmy award for sports broadcasting against favorites Vin Scully (Dodgers) and Mel Allen (Yankees).

As Dick walked to the stage to receive his Emmy, he could only think of his dad, who had passed away that week. Backstage, as he held his award, Johnny Bench approached him, aware of his mourning. "Now you know how it feels to hit a home run, to win the World Series," he told Dick, putting his arm around him. And that's why Johnny Bench was his favorite athlete: "He helped me truly redefine winning as being more than a box score, or numbers; it is the heart of winning that truly matters, and lives on, and creates real legacy."

LEADING FROM THE MIDDLE

Power to grow and make change lies in the middle of the organization, its core, its heart. The head shapes our directions and strives to stay on top. The heart shapes how we feel, receive and act on the world, and it is where all the work gets done. I want to be a voice for that from-the-heart style of leadership.

I lead sales people and sales managers in daily discussions with hospitals, payers, and physicians. I am called a trainer. Today I focus more on the fascinating areas of management and leadership training. We grow sales success through improved coaching and recruiting.

I am throwing out the term "class" in describing our training events. "Class" raises images of a schoolmarm who scolds those under her control, lecturing them into intelligence. Learning today involves standing up and moving around, laughing, challenging, and debating. So training classes are now referred to as programs or workshops or sessions or courses or roundtables.

Training seems to be what people do when they are in a new job or role, or when they need correction to some aspect of their actions. "Let's send them to training," their supervisors say.

Training is more. Much more. It is the development of people. Training goes beyond manuals, modules, slide decks of data and information. Training shapes the culture. Training shapes how we get answers, ask questions, learn, share, and grow. Our ability to adapt, whether as a corporation, or a family, is what helps us to be successful in the face of change, or crisis.

In this book, I will devote a chapter to each letter of the word "leadership." Throughout those chapters, you will notice three core anchors—trust, attitude, and influence—with an abundance of stories that illustrate the building of those anchors.

MY VOICE OF INFLUENCE

When Teri was dying, I found my voice of influence in the hospital. Three doctors and several nurses were sharing with me their thoughts on what I should do for Teri. They were giving me information and asking me to decide. I felt far from qualified to make these critical calls, so I asked them all to join me in the conference room. I introduced myself, and I pointed out that the goal was to do what was best for Teri. I asked them all to discuss what I should do, and then to select someone to come to me and share the consensus, and once that was clearly stated, I would follow it.

My voice of influence had become strained through sadness and confusion. When I found it, the direction was clear: no more surgery for Teri, and she would have fortified antibiotics. Surgery only would painfully prolong the outcome that we knew was inevitable—and that came, six days later. My wife was 41.

We all talk about our favorite scenes in the movies. The sad ones come so often to mind, though even in the sad movies, we find ourselves quoting the funny lines, the quirky moments. We remember, in vivid detail, the life stories played out on the movie screen, the comedies and the tragedies, and the ones that are both. Most movies have a lesson at the core. In all of my own favorites, that lesson, in some way, is one of leadership. I think of Geena Davis in *A League of Their Own*, Tom Hanks in *Apollo 13*, Richard Gere in *Pretty Woman*, and Al Pacino in *Scent of a Woman*.

Do we measure that leadership in success, or in significance? In church one day, our pastor pointed out that we all are significant. It seems people tend to think about "significance" in terms of how well they have amassed wealth to reach their financial goals. True, the Trumps of this world have been significant figures. But there is significance too in that poor soul who gives the last few dollars of his bus money to the offering plate and humbly walks home. That's significance ahead of success.

AT THE CORE OF LEADERSHIP

In today's society, it seems people are considered professional if they have initials behind their names, whether MD, or JD, or DDS, or CPA. Those who aren't professionals go into some other field, such as sales. It's considered by many a place to start. That perception persists: if you aren't smart—if you don't have those initials after your name—you just aren't professional.

In my experience, I have come to understand that true professionalism lies more in how we deal with others. People think of consultants as professional, for example. If you ask for words describing a consultant, people say "smart," and "good listener," and "counselor." Or if you ask how they would describe a "partner," they say "trustworthy," and "friendly," and talk of someone who is "collaborative." Partners know how to deal with others. They know how to appeal to them.

From that viewpoint, sales leaders can be among the PhDs of our world. And yet when you ask people the words that come to mind when they think of the word "salespeople" (Dan Pink asked this question of over 7,000 people and not one thought of sales women, only salesmen), they come up with "greedy," and "pushy," and "deceptive," and the like. It's little wonder that the business cards of people in sales careers identify them as account executive, consultant, business manager, territory manager—anything but salesperson. So much depends on perception, and that's true for leadership of all stripes.

In the 30 years that I have observed management and leadership, however, I have concluded that we are clearly in a leadership void. It is for that reason that I hope to reach out to families: the parents, and also the children who are learning about life. I want to reach out to teachers, those in the classroom, and all who can help us discover our significance and humanity.

Leadership, in short, isn't just for the generals. Rather, it is our daily effort to support our beliefs and values. When it comes to leadership, in a multitude of disciplines, we all need to become professionals. We need to know how to deal squarely and fairly with others. That requires far more than intellect.

It requires the kind of heart that was found in Herb Brooks, the coach of the 1980 Olympic hockey team. Twenty years earlier, in 1960, he was cut from the gold-medal team by a coach who opted instead to include a star player's brother so that the star wouldn't quit. Brooks felt dejected, particularly as he and his father watched the gold go to the USA team over the Soviets in what has been called the "miracle on ice." His father turned to him and said: "Well, I guess they cut the right guy!"

You might understand why Brooks was determined to win gold in 1980: to prove to everyone that he belonged. Whatever his motivation, it shaped his reputation as a coach. Years later, when Brooks died, the entire winning team came to the funeral. The goalie, Jim Craig, explained that each player probably felt Brooks liked him best. He had the ability to make everyone feel special, and he knew how to get the best out of each. Herb's relentless drive, Craig said, only served to galvanize the team on a common mission, to show that they had it in them to do even better. He led with heart.

I want to tell you that we all can do even better. To get to the core of leadership, we need to peel down through the layers of our lives. At the core of an apple are the seeds. At the core of our bodies is the heart. The seed is the essence of the apple, and the heart is the essence of our humanity, and in both lie the promise of new growth.

Chapter 1

LEADING IS LEARNING

"Get busy living or get busy dying!"

—Tim Robbins,
in *Shawshank Redemption* (story by Stephen King)

T hink, for a moment, about your worst supervisor ever, someone whose performance you felt was poor. Now think about your greatest supervisor. You might use the same measures to grade those supervisors. Some of the criteria might be:

- Do they care about their work?

- Do they care about you and other employees?

- Do they treat others fairly, and with respect?

- Do they motivate with praise?

- Do they micromanage?

■ Do their actions lead to absenteeism?

Now grade your own work performance under each of those supervisors, on a scale of 10 percent to 100 percent productivity. Do you find that your performance was dramatically better under a good supervisor? The supervisor's quality may be the only reason for the difference, and that is the essence of this book. Leadership matters.

And it is not defined by one's title. Rather, it comes from how one engages and influences others in achieving personal and organizational goals. You can be a powerful leader whether you are a CEO or unemployed.

Good leaders don't try to mold you to be just like them. Some leaders think that is their job. They believe that the only way to make you capable of taking on advanced tasks and one day filling their shoes is to make every effort to transform you into a copy of themselves. Big mistake. We must be authentic to ourselves and not try to fake it to be like someone else. With some leaders, it seems that everything they do is designed to tell you how far you will have to go to be as good as them.

The leadership demonstrated by your best supervisor made you more productive than the leadership demonstrated by your poorest supervisor. In my own research involving hundreds of people over ten years, I have found that productivity improves by more than 60 percent under a good leader, as compared with a poor leader. That's significant.

THE ROI OF DEVELOPING LEADERS

When it comes to spending money on leadership development and training, one might ask what the ROI is. Well, what's the ROI if we don't develop leaders? Perhaps it is best measured by subtracting that 60 percent boost in productivity and results. These days I talk to management about return on expectations (ROE). Leadership training and development is about improving our perspective, so we have better actions. We measure actions though customer and employee surveys, 360s, and engagement results. "Return on investment" (ROI) is a hard-goods term, and is not designed to measure the "trust" and "professionalism" that appears on so many company mission statements. We acknowledge these traits and there is no way to measure the ROI of training to improve, except through observation and rear-view-mirror feedback of customers and employees. I say, let's identify what behaviors we want to demonstrate "trust," and let's lay out a plan to get there. That's return on expectation, not hours trained, but, rather, behaviors observed.

Leadership matters in all that we do. In a business, leadership results in higher quality and reduced costs. In a family, leadership is the mark of a good parent. A good leader uses time wisely and efficiently. That means less wasted time on the job, and more quality time at home. And leadership is more than being strict or permissive, more than being judgmental or judged. It is measured in the way we touch our values.

Some great leaders will run a business into the ground. Some great parents raise children who contribute less to society or to the family than others. We cannot judge leaders by results alone, as results measure achievement to goal. Results may or may not reflect values. Nor do people's actions necessarily reveal their intentions.

And leadership does not depend upon title, or the power that one person holds over another. Rather, leadership is far more personal, as measured in how the leader supports and directs followers' activities. Business leaders drive results when they influence employees to be more involved and interested. A worker who is 100 percent engaged provides a better return on his salary than one who is only 40 percent engaged. The employer saves time, energy, and money.

In 2000 the New England Patriots football team traded away a first-round draft pick to the New York Jets for the right to acquire Bill Belichick, the Jets' defensive coordinator. That was the first time an NFL football franchise traded away a draft pick for the chance to acquire a coach. Coaching matters: Belichick assumed responsibilities for the head coaching duties and has had remarkable success, taking the Patriots to five Super Bowl appearances and three victories.

Leadership success is often measured by bottom-line success: the increasing stock price, the Super Bowl victory, the Olympic gold, the world title. However, winning is more than the score, and leadership is more, as well. It should be measured more by the influence and power passed on to another. Surviving and dealing with crisis may be a more admirable measure of leadership. And those are skills learned from life.

LEARNING TO LEAD MYSELF

I had had my first job, which I loved, for only six months, and was about to be fired. When I was hired, my boss told me I was a risk: "You have no experience, so don't let us down." Fresh out of school, I worked hard, listened, and learned as fast as I could. Selling was new to me, but I was getting it and enjoying my new role. I had my own apartment, a new TV, and a hibachi. Life was good.

And then one morning, at a regional sales meeting at my three-month mark, our sales team of eight huddled with the boss, who read the results out loud for the quarter. "Rob, 110 percent. Dave, 108 percent, Mike 107 percent…"

The second to last number was 97 percent, and then the boss looked at me. "And you. You're last, at 74 percent." I got a long glare, and then we disbanded.

My second quarter wasn't much better, and I went to more training, in California. I passed all the tests, and in the debrief, the head of sales training gave me the feedback on my week in the home office.

After several very nice comments, he paused. "What seems to be the matter? You seem distracted or not interested. Do you want this feedback?" I explained that I had been told I had six months to improve results, and it had now been over eight months, and I didn't expect to be there the next quarter.

"I don't know what you were told," he said, "but if you can do in the field the things you showed us here that you can do and are interested in doing, then let the numbers take care of themselves. Just keep doing what you're doing, and you should be fine."

I took the advice, and one year later I was runner-up for rookie of the year, and two years later I was number one in the region and number two in the nation. Soon after, I moved into the training area, with that director of training as my boss, who emerged a mentor and encourager at a time when I felt lost, and he was still one of my all-time best mentors 35 years later. I learned how to truly try to be more a person of value, to myself and others.

As a new sales manager, I had just hired the top graduate of our training program when she called me to say she was resigning. The job required too much travel, and she was going back to nursing. I didn't have a backup, and that meant I would fall short of my goals for turnover and vacancies on the very week I submitted them. I scolded her, suggesting she had lied to me about her interest in the job.

I called my boss, Ed, to tell him what had happened and how upset I was about it. This wouldn't happen again, I assured him, and I would meet those goals, and—.

He stopped me. "Jim, in situations like this, honey works better than vinegar, and you are pouring on the vinegar. That's not good for anyone. Settle down." He helped me find the focus that I badly needed.

One winter day in Cleveland, many years later, I was on the phone with my boss, whose name is also Jim, in California. I told him that Fred, one of my managers, was doing a poor job of leading, and his team was frustrated and disengaged, with weak results. He had just screwed up a major account call, and I also found him personally annoying.

I went into a rant with my boss about Fred, after which he had this to say to me, slowly and clearly: "Jim, I am not going to consider you successful at leading people until I can see that you have people you don't like who still are being their most productive."

Whoa! That stopped me in my tracks. And it is so true. It gets back to considering intentions and not judging actions. I'm sure that

Fred hadn't been running home at night to his family, and saying, "Boy, what a loser I am, and I sure upset my boss and team today!"

I realized nothing was going to change until I changed. I needed to act as if Fred was my best employee, and best friend, and treat him the way I treated my favorite team members. While results were slow to improve, they did improve. Fred only reported to me a little while longer due to realignments. I mentored him later on additional challenges he had with management, and our friendship grew. I still think about that day when my boss told me, so clearly, that when you want something to change, it's you who needs to change. Or, as expressed in the famous lectures of Giovanni Livera, "No change, no change!"

ARE YOU ON THE WRONG LADDER?

I had a new manager, Suzanne, who was the best interview candidate I'd seen in a long time. She was well suited to achieve the goals I had for leading a new region. She lasted six months! I was unable to properly onboard her, and set expectations, as Teri's illness required me to be at home and the hospital a great deal. Then Teri passed, and I was gone a lot more. When I returned to see how my team was doing in my absence, and I heard quickly how Suzanne was not excelling, and in fact was way under-performing. So, with energy and focus I set to improve Suzanne's results. I learned you can't improve what someone doesn't know needs improving. And after several weeks of frustrating meetings and clear lack of understanding, I had to do something.

I went to Suzanne's office, and asked, "Can we review all the things that are on our to-do list?" So we amassed a large list on my wallboard, and I said, "Wow, that is a daunting list. How do you think we should go about getting these things done?" She said, "Whoa, I don't know—that's a lot!" I said, "I was actually thinking this is your to-do list." She gave me a blank stare and said, "Really?"

After we talked about some of the projects, I asked her to take a walk. I asked her to take me back to our interviews and to a few months earlier, and compare what she was doing in her last job to what she was doing now. What was the difference? She told me all the things she liked doing and how different the expectations were for this job. I was so impressed with her credentials, I didn't actually check into her work activities and behaviors. Big mistake. In her previous job, in a much bigger company, she was surprised how she had to do so many small tasks that she had never done in her old job. I should have set expectations and interviewed around those. I let her down. I missed. It caused me setbacks in my performance and team goals. It set her back in her career, and she was embarrassed. A very costly learning, and a regret, I have tried to learn from going forward.

I ran into Suzanne, a few years later. She was running her own company, and I accepted full responsibility for her not having a better experience in my organization. While she was polite and cordial, scars only fade, they do not disappear.

We have grown up learning to be corrected, graded, and ranked in all forms of competition. How do we measure learning? On written tests, it is easy, so that becomes the measure. The critical qualities of true leadership—trust, listening, and caring, for example—are harder to measure.

We grow up getting the best grades, getting into the best colleges, getting the best job, all measured by paying the most money and working as hard as we can to retire as early as we can so we can then have fun. We all know people who feel unfulfilled at work, or unsatisfied, despite having applied much effort. They have cars, houses, and vacations, and more wealth than 99.9 percent of the world, and yet they are unhappy. Having climbed the corporate ladder, they have reached unhappiness.

Leadership is about learning what's really important to us—in our heart—and not trying to measure success and happiness by our grades, or our money.

Not long ago, I faced my own crisis of leadership and a new kind of reality. I watched my life go from turbo-charged to neutral. I had felt that climbing the corporate ladder was the goal, and I began realizing through life experiences that my ladder must be misplaced or missing. I started professional selling at 22 years of age, post college graduation. I was leading a team of 10 people by age 26, and running a region of 150 people before my thirtieth birthday. Man, I was cruising into the boardroom.

From age 30 to age 40, I traveled nonstop, determined to whip my team into shape and get the next big sale to make my region number one. As my family started to grow, and the needs at home mounted, I found myself stalling, trying to be everywhere and do everything. Although I said my family was most important, I wasn't showing that, based on the time, money, and effort that I was applying to my work as opposed to my family.

My values and desires were not balanced. Making my boss happy and making my home life happy were in constant misalignment. And I smiled at everyone, saying that everything was great. I found myself not being promoted as fast as I was earlier. Business changes and shifts in leadership were making that mountain even taller to climb—in my eyes. My family was in Cleveland, which is buried in snow eight months of the year, and I was often on the road. When I was home, I was on the phone, and with my company headquartered on the West Coast, a 5 p.m. conference call for my leadership team was bath time and bedtime in my Cleveland home.

I was unhappy and still trying to be the extroverted optimist, telling everybody I was happy. I recall one time "coming clean" with my boss, at my performance review, telling him that in my career I wanted three things:

1. to stay with my company—great products, people, future, leadership team, customers;

2. to stay in Ohio—I had family there, and it was great for my wife and kids;

3. to get off the road—heavy travel was taking a toll, and I needed to become more involved in the community and cultivate friends.

Without much hesitation, he said, "Jim, I can get you any two of those, and not all three." So, I took 1 and 3. I stayed with my company and moved to the home office to get off the road. And I said goodbye to Ohio. I based my move on my values, on my desire to be at home more with my family. I sacrificed the geography, and doing a job that I enjoyed and in which I felt valued and productive.

I have shared with many people over the years, as they contemplate difficult career and family moves, the importance of starting with a deep introspective look at personal values. Who are we really? What will our tombstones say? What do we really want, for ourselves, not based on what others want from us? Then, knowing our values, we make our decisions to stay or go, to start or stop. If we base our actions on our values and on learning about ourselves, we win, regardless of the short- or long-term outcome. That is the right decision.

Sometimes as we try to advance in the corporate rat race, it feels as if we are crawling on a spider web rather than climbing a ladder. (Funny how I got the words "rat" and "spider" in the same sentence to describe the corporate career path!) We come to suspect that we're on the wrong ladder when someone asks, "Why are you so angry?" or tells us that we seem short-tempered. That perspective may be difficult to accept when it comes from our boss. So, we compensate by working harder to prove we can do the impossible. Or we seem obsessed with the trappings of achievement, knowledge, power, or admiration.

TO GROW, WE MUST LEARN

In truth, however, the changes we seek and the success we crave will come from our capacity to learn. And we do crave change. We talk openly with one another at work and at home about all the things we want to change. We want a change in our income, and in how we manage our time, and we want to find out how to get others to do the things we want them to do.

We must learn how something works and also why. The "why" of people can be the most significant: Why did they say that? Why are they always acting that way? There are reasons: the way they were raised, perhaps, or how they learned to process the world. We all process our world differently, with different beliefs and values. If we are to improve our surroundings, we will have our greatest opportunity to do so once we understand how we came to process the world.

Our ability to learn is our only real advantage as we strive to advance ourselves and grow. Whether we start off as a child of privilege or as a child of a desperate situation, we will require learning if we are to grow. We will need to learn from our mistakes as well as from our successes. So often we stumble through life, convinced that, "Well, these are the cards I was dealt, and so I'm just doing the best I can."

To do our very best, though, we will need some introspection. Is it really the very best that we can do? What are our goals? We need goals and vision to determine whether we are performing at the optimum level, and in setting goals we need to ask a few questions of ourselves:

- What do I want to be good at?

- What do I like doing and want to get better at?

- What do other people need that I can help to fulfill?

When talents and enthusiasm overlap with a need, that's the recipe for success. And success is ours if, along the way, we adjust, based on learning from our actions.

Mistakes are the bridge between experience and wisdom. When asked, during his research, if he had been disappointed when all his initial attempts to create a light bulb produced no results, Thomas Edison said, "Why, man, I have gotten a lot of results! I know several thousand things that won't work."

In the movie *The Shawshank Redemption*, Morgan Freeman plays a prison inmate who, at the outset, declares that after 15 years, "I'm a changed man. I'm no longer a danger to society." He was denied parole. Later, after 40 years in jail, he says, "I look back on the way

I was then: a young, stupid kid who committed that terrible crime. I want to talk to him. I want to try and talk some sense to him, tell him the way things are. But I can't. That kid's long gone and this old man is all that's left." His parole was approved.

Our greatest learning comes when we are the most vulnerable and honest, and our greatest moments of leadership comes when all that baggage is gone.

Mark Twain said that when he was 14, he considered his father ignorant, and he marveled at how much the old man learned in the next seven years. He said, "The older I got, the smarter he got." Leadership is best learned by living and doing, and we don't need the podium or pulpit to display that leadership. We need to move around, get the blood flowing, and get to work. We retain only a fraction of what we read, more of what we practice, and if we teach others what we have learned, we have the best chance of learning our lessons well.

FOCUS ON WHAT YOU DO BEST

Our talent and intellect and enthusiasm shape our personal and professional development plans. Those plans first require us to look inside ourselves and create a personal success map. We can write them down and discuss them with others to see how the plans feel and sound. That way we can make adjustments and reprioritize. Our plans are tools for learning and growing.

Years ago, my supervisor told me, "Jim, here are several things you do well, and there are a number of things you need to do better. So, we'll put this development plan together to help you get *good* at these things that you are *not good* at doing." So, over the years we built elaborate plans of SMART goals, meaning specific, measurable, actionable, realistic, and time-bound goals.

How often did I go back and review these goals? As often as my boss wanted to review them—yearly. He knew it was not fun for either of us to review areas in which I didn't really have an interest in getting better. In my case, it was financial analysis. I completed courses in finance for the nonfinancial manager. I didn't have the talent or enthusiasm for financial analysis. I was not going to become an expert in this area. At best, I could be competent. My interest in those development plans waned quickly.

I learned to stop beating my head into the wall because my boss told me to do something or because I felt I should follow the obvious career path as presented in a company manual. Rather, when my boss and I got to areas I needed to improve, I applied appropriate effort to be competent in those areas and focused the larger part of my time and energy on areas in which I was already good, with a goal to become an expert, master, teacher of others, and champion of my own good skills. I had latent talent and enthusiasm for certain activities, and when I was applying myself to those areas, I frankly had more success, fun, and personal sense of achievement. One learns best where one finds passion.

ONE GOLF BALL AT A TIME

In 1954, as he neared the end of his career, Einstein was a professor at Princeton. He needed to relax, and was encouraged to take up golf. So, he took golf lessons, and as many golfers quickly come to realize, golf and relaxation rarely work well in the same sentence. Einstein's golf instructor was providing loads of information to him on how to stand, bring up the club, follow through, and so on. Einstein was soon frustrated and stopped the lesson. He turned to his instructor, and said, "Let me show you something." And he bent down and picked up four golf balls, and he said to the instructor, "I would appreciate it, as I toss these to you, that you catch them." And as he tossed all four balls at once, the instructor did not catch any. Einstein then bent over, and picked up one golf ball and said, "Let's try again." This time he tossed only one ball, which the instructor caught. As the instructor stared at Einstein, the scientist said, "I cannot learn all the information, just because you say it. I need to practice one thing at a time to learn, not just be thrown information."

Chapter 2

EMPATHY AND GIVING BACK

"See the world from someone else's viewpoint and you just may see your world from a fresh perspective"

—Dorothy Carlson,
Ragan Communications, *Bits and Pieces on Leadership*

"Is that really what I want?" we often ask ourselves. If we take inventory of all the blessings and all things great and small in our lives, do we really want all of them?

I drive past many houses with garages full of stuff that needs to be cleaned out every few years. When sellers get money from garage sales, they buy more stuff with the proceeds, use it once, and store it for the next garage sale. Packrats everywhere have heard the resounding cry from those more inclined to throw things away: "You have never even used that. So get rid of it!"

Are all those things really so important? If someone asks us what's most important to us, the response usually includes family, faith, joy, and love. And "love" applies in both our personal and business lives. It's the love of what we do that brings us success, not the success of our deeds that brings us love.

OUR NEEDS AND OUR WANTS

Here are some of the things that we might get when we are successful in our pursuits:

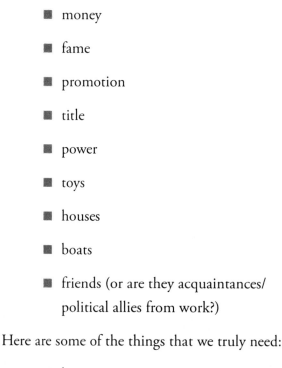

- money

- fame

- promotion

- title

- power

- toys

- houses

- boats

- friends (or are they acquaintances/ political allies from work?)

Here are some of the things that we truly need:

- love

- hope

- joy

- trust

- integrity

- friends (trusted partners)

- praise

- fun

- freedom

- sincerity

- faith

- peace

"We buy things we don't need, with money we don't have, to impress people we don't know," says Rick Warren, author of *The Purpose Driven Life* and pastor at Saddleback Church in Lake Forest, California.

The terms in those lists are pretty much self-explanatory, though I'll tell you a story about the difference between "friends" and "trusted partners." At a presentation that I gave a few years ago, a gentleman in the front row asked me if I knew the difference. And in his thick southern Alabama accent, he told me, "Well, boy, if you were to accidently kill somebody, a friend would stand beside you all the way. But, a partner—well, they'd actually help you bury the body!"

So, try doing a quick inventory of where you spend your time, money, and energy. Do you focus on your wants or on your needs? Most of us are so busy getting the things we want that we miss getting the things we say we stand for. We say it is important to be a good husband, wife, son, friend, parent, yet we are losing our values at work and at home in the interest of getting what we want.

We want the world a certain way—our way—and we get disappointed when it is not. We need to learn the art of empathy; that is, putting ourselves in others' shoes, and striving to understand what they want and need. That's different from sympathy, which is agreeing with someone's feelings. Empathy is simply acknowledging those feelings, whether of sadness or joy. If you sympathize with colleagues, you are taking their side in the situation. You are aligned mentally and emotionally. If you empathize, however, you recognize the feelings, regardless of the reason for them. Leaders do not need to sympathize, but they certainly must empathize if they are to be effective.

A LITTLE ACT OF KINDNESS

When I was growing up, I loved baseball, and in particular, my Cincinnati Reds. At age seven or eight, I knew all the players, collected their baseball cards, listened to games on my transistor radio, and pretended to be certain players in backyard, pick-up baseball games with my friends. One day my mom and dad took me to a local department store (remember those?) where the great Frank Robinson was signing autographs. Frank was a great outfielder and hitter, and he was one on my favorite players. Quiet, soft-spoken Frank was every kid's favorite! I was so excited that I took my glove and wore my Little League jersey and Cincinnati reds cap, and I brought along his baseball card and some paper for him to sign.

When we got there, he was standing on a small stage in a suit and tie, in front of all these kids, and he looked like a king! He spoke and then signed autographs. So many kids and so little time. I was sure I'd never get to see him up close or get an autograph. He looked tired as the crowd of kids moved me closer. He had been there far longer than had been scheduled, and I thought he was about ready to leave. I was starting to feel discouraged. My dad encouraged me to be patient and keep moving forward (good advice for all time).

When I got to the front, Frank looked at me, and he started to hand me an autographed photo of himself. Before I accepted it, I pulled out his baseball card, which I cherished, and looked at it and then at him, and I said: "Here, Mr. Robinson, this is for you." He looked at the card a little surprised and smiled. With bright, quiet, and sensitive eyes, and a warm smile, he said: "Thank-you very much!" I collected his autograph and said good-bye.

His look as he accepted my act of kindness has never left me. He was genuinely surprised and touched. Everybody else came that day to get a piece of Frank, and I gave him something: a smile. Today I tip too much, I look for the good too often, and I find ways to do the little things to make somebody smile, all in an effort to see that same look one more time on somebody's face as I saw that day 45 years ago on Frank Robinson's face.

It was the simple gratitude of a smile or bright eye that recognizes and appreciates that somebody else is trying to be kind when it's least expected...

GIVING MEANS GETTING

So how do you get those things that are more important to your definition of you and your real success?

Give it away!

If you want more of the things that you need, you have to give those things. It is that simple.

It seems to make no sense. From earliest childhood we are conditioned to believe certain things: "Good things come to those who work hard." "Nice guys finish last." "The early bird gets the worm." "Winning is not the most important thing; it's the only thing."

What we truly need will come to us as we give to others. I'm not talking about dispensing your unsolicited advice, intellect, direction, perspective, and counsel to others. I'm talking about truly giving of ourselves.

THE HERO OF THE HUDSON

Ric Elias, who was a passenger on the U.S. Airways plane that crashed into the Hudson River in 2010, remarked that, as a survivor, he decided to cherish relationships. He said he has chosen to be happy, not right. His ego had gotten in the way, he said, and he thought of all the time he wasted trying to be right about things that didn't matter instead of spending time with the people who did matter.

If we give unconditionally of our time to help people just because they need it, not because we want to feel good about helping, we will receive a gift in return. We will gain some of the things we truly need. By giving away time, money, and energy, great gifts come back to us: We become better bosses, employees, friends, and parents. We become increasingly able to fully engage with others, viewing our time with them not as an interruption or distraction but as an opportunity to reach out to a fellow human being. People become more important to us than tasks.

THE EFFECT ON THE BOTTOM LINE

A landscaping nursery in Victorville, California, decided it was time to do something to help its employees. They had been potting plants and using a lot of manure, and the acidic soil was causing problems for their hands and skin. The nursery management reasoned that much of the problem was because the manure had been getting wet in the rain, so they began putting tarps over the manure to keep it dry. And soon the nursery was experiencing a 55 percent increase in yield. Why? The wet manure had been clumping, making it hard for plant roots to grow. Now, with dry soil, the plants were thriving. Management had not understood why so many plants had been failing.

The lesson: Taking care of your employees can lead directly to increased productivity and results.

THE BOY AND THE BRICK WALL

Management expert Ken Blanchard talks about the secrets of leadership, and emphasizes the importance of servant-leadership. I think of the story of a small boy who'd been injured badly in a car accident, and his family was gone. As he suffered in a hospital, unable to move, with broken legs, he would sometimes get visitors, including an older gentleman who would stop by to chat with him and listen. The boy would ask the old man, "What's going on out that window over there?" And the old man would look out the window and tell him about all the people with their packages, and all the bustle and traffic on a sunny day. After a few weeks, the old man stopped coming. The boy was told he had passed away. The boy was determined to gain the strength to get out of bed and look out the window for himself, and after a month, he did. He looked out the window, and down—and he saw a brick wall. The old man had given the boy a vision of what might be. He offered inspiration, in the true spirit of a servant-leader.

THE VINTNER'S FAVORITE WINE

I had the opportunity several years ago to visit a winemaker up in Napa, and as the winemaker was explaining how the grapes and the wine and the temperature and the soil were put together to build a great wine, one of the members of my group said to this young man, the vintner, "What's your favorite wine?" And without much thought, after all the science we'd been discussing about soil testing and temperatures, he said, "That's pretty easy for me."

"A few months ago," he explained, "I had the chance to join my fiancée on a Friday night out here in Napa at a little restaurant that we'd never been to before. It was old and rickety but had a great, big, old deck, and we sat out on a warm Friday evening with the sunset casting across the vineyards a beautiful array of greens and yellows, and we sat there that evening and planned our wedding and celebrated a beautiful week, and were drinking a bottle of red wine. I have absolutely no idea who made that wine, and today it's my favorite."

It's not about just the results that we attain; it's more about the journey, and the differences that we make to people as we go forward. What we can give to others along the way is, in large part, the measure of our leadership.

Chapter 3

ACTION AND PEOPLE

"If we are patient in a moment of anger, we
will escape a hundred days of sorrow."

—Chinese proverb

I used to have a sign in my office that said: "Patience, my butt. I'm going to go out and kill something." Patience, however, is a virtue. Many of us, however, never put it into action. I've learned that patience and action come together as listening.

It takes restraint and time to listen, when what we really want to do is act. Action seems to be the better use of time. We're getting something done. We value the action as the key to success, hard work, and greater good. In a way, listening is indeed action, and a high form of it. Instead of speaking, we turn on our ears, not to hear the words, necessarily, as much as the intent.

A young boy asked his grandfather why, after so many years, he never had talked about the time he spent in a concentration camp during World War II. "Why?" the old man replied. "It's because they took five years of my life away from me there, and I won't give them one more minute of my time." The lesson: Move forward, and don't look back.

We often mistake activity for achievement. We think that if we are busy, we are moving forward on a course for success. We hear the refrain of our parents' statements as they set up our belief system: "A rolling stone gathers no moss," and, "If at first you don't succeed, try, try again," and, "Success is 10 percent inspiration and 90 percent perspiration."

All these statements feed a growing fire of business that we take to be a visible sign of success. Perhaps you even hang around the office after hours, hoping that some senior manager will walk by and see how busy you are.

That is a big part of the success motif: looking busy. Creating the perception of being a hard worker seems to be a ticket to the next promotion. At what costs do we create that perception?

In 1950 it was virtually impossible to work a 24-hour day. The business shut down at 5 p.m. and the doors closed, and everyone went home. They went home to newspapers, radio, or three channels of TV. The children of the '50s were told that they couldn't go out to play until they had finished their homework, and there were no snacks or dessert until after dinner. They were conditioned and disciplined to complete all their work before they could enjoy themselves. With today's technology, there is no finish line to the work. How, then, does one relax and enjoy life?

The formula for success is the same as the formula for a nervous breakdown. If you want to work a 24-hour day, you can with the help of the Internet, 24-hour global television, distance-based education, self-help programs, and web links to a world of never-ending activity.

A LESSON FROM SPORTS SCIENCE

Before the development of sports science, top athletes typically were urged to push harder and train longer. Little time was allotted for recovery. The same can be said of employees today who work harder, longer and without sufficient recovery, just to get the job done.

There has to be a better way. For athletes, the outcome was often anxiety, depression, injury and other symptoms of stress. For 54 percent of American workers, it means disengagement from work (according to research conducted by the Gallup Organization, 2010) and similar symptoms of stress. The results have been shortened careers and lifelong health issues for athletes, and burnout as well as both physical and emotional health issues for the employees of today.

Sports science has combined the disciplines of exercise physiology, nutrition, psychology, biomechanics, motor learning, and sports medicine, and its application has resulted in an incredible progression in athletic performance during the last 40 years. Athletes are typically bigger, faster, stronger, and more emotionally resilient. They eat better and recapture energy quickly to perform well the next day.

Applying the principles of sports science, employees of the future should see themselves as multidimensional and ensure that they get adequate recovery in each dimension. Chronic stress—that is, stress without recovery—can lead to health complications and impact performance. Just like an athlete, the employee needs to replenish energy in the form of sleep, hydration, nutrition, and physical activity.

In addition, employees should be encouraged to balance work with rest. For example, taking short breaks during the day, disconnecting from work on weekends, and truly enjoying earned vacation time. Intentional downtime, even as short as one or two minutes, enables us to come back stronger when we get to work. Businesses that take a page from the world of sports science and deploy a multidimensional approach to employee performance can help improve productivity, innovations, and engagement.

LEADERSHIP IS ABOUT PEOPLE, NOT TASKS

We have so many tasks to complete that we can forget that leadership and real success involves dealing with people. We get so busy multitasking and dealing with daily activities that we disregard people. We feel compelled to be in action mode every day.

I was recently in an elevator with another person when the doors opened and a young woman joined us. She was talking on a cell phone. As she continued to talk, she pushed the buttons for several floors and then turned to us and apologized, explaining that she was multitasking and had pushed those buttons without thinking. The elevator rose one floor and she got off, still talking on her phone. The other passenger and I just shrugged as we stopped at the next several floors, waiting for the doors to open and close. Plenty of action, slow progress.

Several years ago, a young minister was trying to come up with a sermon and found himself really struggling to create it. His nine-year-old son came to him with a geography problem and needed his dad's help. The boy had a paper map of the world and said he had to learn the world's major countries and couldn't remember them all. So, the dad took the map and cut it into smaller pieces and, to help his son remember where they all went, suggested his son try to put the puzzle pieces together. After only a few minutes, the young boy came back to his dad and proudly beamed, having put the map together really quickly. The minister asked his son how he had done it so quickly. The boy flipped the map over, and on the back of the map was the face of a boy. The boy said, "I just put the boy together, and the rest of the world fell into place." And his father had the material for his sermon.

Ken Blanchard says we should focus not on "getting work done through people" but, rather, on "getting people done through work." I believe the work we do today prepares us through experiences, trials, and failures for the next battle. It seems that work should be more than binders and meetings. Our work day is full of activity that, if properly assessed and harnessed, is simply a proving ground with the potential to improve all kinds of relationships, whether they are customer, colleague, or parental relationships. If we aspire to such values as character, integrity, trust, and honesty in our family and professional lives, we need to start building those relationships. That's what will grow our productivity and outcomes and financial ratios. We cannot win simply by pushing harder. We need to stop pushing employees and customers and families, and instead we should pull them toward us.

DEVELOPING RELATIONSHIPS

In dealing with people, leadership authority Stephen Covey says, "If you want to save time, don't be efficient with people." Although you can be efficient with your actions, you need an intimate approach to human beings. "With people," Covey emphasizes, "slow is fast and fast is slow."

Journalist and speaker Malcolm Gladwell reported that in 1960 teenagers spent 40 percent of their time with adults. In 1990 they spent 30 percent of their time with adults. By 2000 that statistic had fallen to 20 percent. And what might that figure be now?

We wonder why youth cannot seem to handle the pressures of society. Instead of learning from those with experience, they are learning life from videos, peers, and the Internet. I read recently that driver education and training schools find that they need to teach today's teenagers more of the fundamentals about steering and dealing with traffic. Reason: Many teenagers have never ridden a bike or had any experience in navigating in traffic. Steering for baby boomers was a simple conversion from handlebar to steering wheel. Today's young drivers haven't made that connection.

Six out of ten Americans do not know their neighbors' names. Of those who know their neighbors, four out of ten have never borrowed anything from them, not even a cup of sugar. Asked why they haven't built relationships with their neighbors, most give the reason that they are too busy.

Technology was designed to make our jobs easier, and it seems to have led to even more challenges. Smart phones and handheld computers, e-mailing and texting have made our dealings with people faster—and that means slower. Technology is pulling us farther away from one another. No wonder we are challenged in our actions.

A TALE OF TWO COACHES

Leaders' actions often look different in the face of getting results. Take Bobby Knight and John Wooden, both highly successful college basketball coaches. Bobby Knight, at Indiana University and Texas Tech, and John Wooden, the Wizard of UCLA, possess talent, fundamentals, drive for success, and national championship success, and they differed greatly in their treatment of their players.

John Wooden once said that if a player is able to make a three-point shot and misses it in the final seconds of a close game, the coach has done something wrong. He had a high sense of responsibility for not over-coaching or under-coaching his team. If the results weren't what he wanted or what had been demonstrated could be done, he reviewed his own actions. He didn't blame the players. John Wooden was an easily loved coach.

Bobby Knight was fiery. Hot tempered, he yelled at players, pushed them, scolded and berated them, and was far less easy to love. Still, both coaches had many players who loved them, depending upon what they needed from their coach.

In the twenty-first century the leadership lessons of John Wooden will set the standard for future success, while Bobby Knight most likely will be a reflection of the great results of yesteryear. The Wooden model of leadership will prevail. Wooden emphasized that his ultimate goal was not building great basketball teams and players. Rather, he said, he was building great citizens through basketball.

THE RULE OF 5 AND 50

As author Marshall Goldsmith explains, when you correct people, you can add 5 percent more value to their project—and you also hurt their commitment to the project by as much as 50 percent. Consider this: When you read a document that states, "All these things are great," followed by a "but", all the positive things that were stated before the "but" are no longer valuable. The compliments have come at a price.

By simply changing that "but" to "and," you will have much better success. I've learned to eliminate the word "but" from all of my e-mails dealing with people and to use the word "and" instead. The message resonates. You continue to create a positive experience versus one that looks corrective.

A 2007 HBR article by psychologist John Gottmann, PhD, talks about relationships being a "salt shaker of yeses." Expressions such as "Sounds good," "You bet," "Keep it going," "Love it," "Great idea. Let's share it with others. Can you tell me more?" are statements of success that convey "Yes, yes, yes," meaning success. If you want positive movement from people, you need four statements of praise for every statement of criticism. If you tell somebody that they can improve in one area, even if you pay them a compliment, you're not seen as a balanced leader. If you have four statements of praise for each statement of correction, you might have a chance of being perceived as a balanced leader.

ATTITUDE REFLECTS LEADERSHIP

Is your leadership style the mirror or the window? When things go well, do you look in the mirror and say, "Hey! Look at me! Look at how good I am!"? Or do you point out the window and say, "We owe it to each one of them. They're the ones doing it." Ask yourself this: is it only when things are going poorly that you point at others?

Our attitude reflects our leadership. You are one sort of leader if you claim successes for yourself and pin the blame on others. You are another sort entirely if you accept the responsibility and share in the glory. The mark of a good leader is not the results so much as the treatment of people.

LOOKING GOOD! BEING GOOD?

On my team, Greg was a successful guy: determined, smart and highly urgent. He was big on himself, too. He knew he was good, and he wasn't afraid to let you know about his successes. He dressed like a winner and talked like a jerk: so pompous, and so full of himself. I worked with him to tone him down, and clarify how his actions were coming across to others. That didn't seem to work. So I got more forceful and marked him down on his work performance review and found ways to slow field promotions, to punish the behavior I began, not just to dislike, but to become emotional about him not changing. C'mon man, I listen, tell, manage, and to no avail. I realized I wasn't leading him, or shaping what good really looks like.

Janet was in a nearby community to Greg, and she was a solid performer, and not as president's club–focused as Greg. They didn't talk much, as she didn't have much time for his braggadocio and machismo. Her personal time was spent with her mother, who was struggling with post-chemo recovery, and her siblings were plane flights away and of little support. Her husband had been laid off from his machinist's job, and her daughter was struggling and complaining, asking why she hadn't spent more time with Janet's ex-husband since their divorce many years earlier. Janet didn't have time for Greg, and was equally determined to grow her job success. Her job was vitally important to her. I had an idea.

There was an upcoming business conference in St. Louis, hosting discussions of other key business leaders on the topic of winning and success. So I had Greg and Janet go together to the 2 day conference. It meant driving 3 hours together in same car—that was a requirement. They agreed and took off. Upon their return, I ran into them both as they were seeing each other for the first time since the St. Louis conference. I saw smiles and hugs. Never before had I seen Greg greet anyone with affection. He had always seemed to see everyone as a selling target. This wasn't usual. This was two people gaining an appreciation for each other's values. I knew Greg had been hardened over the years, as his father had moved many times, never seeming to find a stable job. Greg hadn't seen his father for 15 years, and proudly would state—"who needs the load: don't know— don't care what he's doing!"

Wow. Greg actually pulled me over at one point in a meeting, and said he learned some things about Janet, I should know. I nodded and listened to every word, as Greg, with compassion and energy, shared with me how tough Janet had it. And he learned all the things I knew—from Greg's perspective. Greg and Janet were much better teammates, from that trip forward. They didn't talk disparagingly about each other as they had in the past. Greg remained competitive and Janet stay focused on her career. They both eventually took their success with my team into other organizations. Janet spent more time in hospice nursing and Greg went onto high-end equipment selling. I ran into a friend, who said their son had Greg as a youth leader at a summer camp, and they loved him.

Learning: stop trying to move people, like pulling or pushing a burro—we move ourselves—just set the right table, and they'll come!

Chapter 4

DECISIONS AND LEARNING FROM QUESTIONS

"It's better to know some of the questions than all of the answers."

—James Thurber

My father suffers from Alzheimer's disease. When I took him to lunch recently, to our favorite Cincinnati chili place, he looked at the menu and just stared into the pages. I asked him what he was going to have, as if I needed to ask! A "three-way" had been his mainstay for years.

With tears in his eyes, he said he couldn't remember how anything tasted and wasn't sure what to order. He'd forgotten taste. Later that week, my mom was upset because my father had forgotten you can't take a shower with slippers on. He writes notes to himself, and he reads them all the time and still doesn't remember why he went upstairs in the first place. He may go to bed for a few hours and then go downstairs for cereal at midnight, thinking it's breakfast time, frustrated that the morning paper isn't there.

Proud and powerful—that's my dad. He rarely cried and never hugged. He told me he loved me, however, and was dedicated to always being home for a family dinner. He was our rock, and he shaped my perception of fairness and honesty. I recall a time when my sister and I teased him as he lost at a board game. "Well, I may be losing, but at least I'm honest," he said, letting us know he'd noticed our taking liberties with the rules. Honesty was his mantra. Without it, he told us, you have nothing.

And I see in this man his honesty even as he passed away, his mental power diminished in his failing years. He didn't complain or yell. He knew, in all honesty, that it was time.

Alzheimer's isn't so much a memory-loss disease as it is a learning disease. The pain is in being unable to learn. If you ever watch a television show to the end, whether a news show or a comedy, or if you read past the headlines in the newspaper, you are learning. With Alzheimer's, you become unable to follow a story, a book, a conversation, a TV show—anything. Learning has ceased.

My mother and sister have given immeasurable love, to support my dad, and myself, as he passed away in 2011. The other day, at a business meeting, I was in another passionate discussion with someone, and as I glanced to my side, I saw myself in the hotel ballroom mirror. I did a double take, and paused. I saw my dad—in me. I didn't used to wear glasses, and with age, I wear glasses more.

My dad wore glasses for years, and in that moment, I almost choked, as I realized I look like my dad. I never really thought about that. He's gone, and I will be too. Time to pay respect back to him, and finish my book.

OUR GREATEST LESSONS

We learn our greatest lessons from our decisions gone bad, or from the questions we ask. A sense of intellectual curiosity propels us into the next great learning experience. And as we discussed in Chapter 1, our learning is the basis for our leadership.

Ask first. Questions might help you reach a decision. In fact, it's the great questions that have more value than the great answers. We learn best when we find the answers on our own rather than merely having them told to us. We learn through our participation in problem solving.

Phil Silvers of 1950s TV comedy shows and Broadway fame was going to visit a friend for the weekend. His friend wanted to get Phil a special gift for their celebration. When Phil drove up in a Rolls Royce Silver Cloud, his friend knew just what to do. He told Phil that the weekend was all planned, and Phil would not need his car, and how about he take the car to his mechanic for a thorough once-over to make sure everything was great. So Phil agreed, and while the car was at the mechanic's, his friend had the car customized top to bottom with a custom bar, TV, VCR, phone system, and stereo. When the car was delivered to Phil Silvers on Monday, they walked toward the car, and his friend suggested Phil look inside to make sure everything was good. Phil's response was, "Oh, I'm sure it's fine; it's just a rental."

Why didn't Phil tell his host earlier that it was a rental? Well, his host never *asked*. He didn't clarify his intent, or ask any questions before jumping into action. Planning is essential for all our actions, to ensure we are achieving our goals. Although Phil's friend wanted to do something special for him, all that time and money did not hit that goal. Because the car was a rental, not only was the value lost on Phil Silvers, but his friend faced the possibility of a run-in with the rental company.

The situation created action in a totally different direction than had been intended. A few questions or observations could have helped avoid this situation, such as, "Hey, nice car! How long have you had this?"

Without clear planning, your results may not be good, and that's particularly the case in the business world. Ask questions. If you ask good questions, the answers will have much to do with the direction you should take.

QUALITY QUESTIONS LEAD TO SOLUTIONS

So why don't we ask better questions? Even weak questions are better than not asking any questions. I've worked with sales people and coaches for years, and the factors that lead to their successes are also involved in derailing their successes. Successful business people—and frankly, all of us—have a desire to look right, or knowledgeable, or professional, or at least not embarrass ourselves.

What happens when we ask a question? Initially, we are seeking knowledge, but we fear that by doing so, we may look less knowledgeable. So we choose to give the impression we know more than we do know. A recent 2005 study by *Harvard Business Review* indicated that 87 percent of business problems were a direct result of poor communication skills rather than the competency or knowledge of either of the parties involved.

DON'T FAKE IT

Even when we get an answer, we may nod and say, "Sure," or "Yeah," or "Okay," but have no idea what really was said. And because we didn't take the time to be clear about the first answer, we ask more questions that can expose our ignorance, and all because we feared a good question might make us look inept. If we ask great questions that lead to great insights, maybe we won't understand the answer. That's embarrassing. For a while, you may create the illusion that you know more than you do—at least in your own perception— and that's not a very productive way to conduct your affairs. With such a strategy, you would be better off not talking. At least that way people might think you know more than you do. Once you open your mouth, you confirm for everyone how little you know.

By contrast, a good question pays dividends. It demonstrates your thirst for knowledge and your willingness to learn from others. Faking it can damage your credibility. However, a good question, well timed, demonstrates confidence and inspires others to view you with respect.

Asking the right questions isn't easy. It is because it is so easy to ask the same question to everyone, versus customizing our questions to the individual in front of us. I had Marshall on my corporate management team, a few years ago. A real go-getter, and ready to take his job to the next level. He was easy to manage, and required little management from me, as he was good at showing me his progress on projects, and was doing a great job.

Or so I thought. I went to a management course, and thought I'd exercise my new learning on Marshall in his next 1:1. So, as part of my learning, to gauge my management style to his stage of learning and competency, I reviewed his projects and how I was managing him. We got to managing some workshops, and I knew he had this, so I said, "This seems to require little from me—you got these, right?" I had never asked that simple question before. He paused and said sheepishly, "Sure." I recognized a lack of confidence, and said, "You got these, right?" He said, "Well I'm not sure about a lot of stuff." So, in my wisdom, I actually challenged him—confirming he should have this! I said things like , "You're just toying with me." I went on to explain why I thought he had the project covered.

And as it turns out he had over the past few weeks, been determined to not show me, his utter frustration. As he revealed to me his really slow progress, and lack of confidence in telling the total truth and status of these projects to me, I was sad: sad I had missed this, and I realized I had totally mis-managed him, to make my life easier.

I had seen success on a smaller scale, and now this project had national implications, and I had done nothing to help him—he never asked for it, and I thought he would ask me, if he needed my help. My bad—we have to make sure our employees' and coworkers' skills are in-line with the result, not fake confidence. I told him, "Marshall, I am so sorry. I've let you down, and I don't know all the answers to your concerns. Together we will figure this out to gain the results we both want."

Immediately his shoulders dropped. The stress he'd been carrying had caused him numerous sleepless nights, and I went to work, listening to other departments, and made sure I helped Marshall, instead of just patting him on the back every day. I was delegating to him, when he needed to learn. I wasn't helping—I was hurting him. He probably told others I was not a good coach. I was telling people I was doing a great job developing people. Wrong. Marshall had been hiding his true feelings, so as not to appear weak. If I had created a safer environment allowing him to be fully honest, the work, results and our relationship would have been better; much better. So easy and so easily missed!

Chapter 5

EARLY VALUES

"We too often sacrifice long term values and greater good, for short term profit and personal gain. The economic collapse of 2008 resulted from a lapse in conscious capitalism."

—Indra Nooyi
CEO, PepsiCo

Although we say that our values are important, we rarely review what they are or what we mean by "values." Let's do an exercise.

Tom Schulte is a friend and the owner of Recalibrate Professional Development. He has built a great values-development program that brings clarity and insight to people and organizations. He uses the chart below.

Let's look at this list and pick the 20 words that you think are your values. Choose the words that describe you or that you hope others use to describe you. These should be the words most likely to describe you in your actions today.

Word	Definition
Balance	Seeking harmony in most aspects of life
Growth	Maturing in lifelong learning, personal development, self-education
Trust	Firm reliance on the integrity, ability, or character of a person or thing
Achievement	Accomplishing the highest levels of excellence
Commitment	Obligation to something greater than one's self
Creativity/Innovation	Imaginative ways of doing things; forming new creations differently
Family	Being with or enjoying quality moments with close relatives
Honesty	The quality or condition of being truthful or sincere
Leadership	The ability to influence others to accomplish something
Appearance	They way one looks or presents oneself to others
Passion	Boundless enthusiasm; strong, enthusiastic devotion to a cause, ideal, or goal
Change	Continuous variety in one's activities; doing things differently
Freedom	The capacity to exercise choice; free will
Accountability	Taking responsibility for one's behaviors and results
Faith/Religion	Belief or action based on a higher power; spirituality
Fun	Focus on enjoyment, amusement, or pleasure
Independence	Freedom from the influence, guidance, or control of another or others; self-reliance
Love	Feelings of deep and tender affection, warmth, and solicitude
Parenting	The rearing of a child or children; care, love, and guidance given by a parent
Integrity	Steadfast adherence to a moral or ethical code; words and deeds matching up

Persistence	Refusing to give up or let go; persevering obstinately
Fitness/Health	Good health or physical condition resulting from exercise and proper nutrition
Respect	The state of being regarded with honor or esteem
Data	Factual information used as a basis for reasoning or discussion
Security	Freedom from doubt, anxiety, or fear; confidence
Loyalty	Feeling or attitude of devoted attachment and affection to a person, cause, or ideal
Status	High standing in one's position; prestige
Volunteerism/Service	Helping or serving others in the community
Career	A chosen pursuit; a profession or occupation
Simplicity	Lack of complexities in life and in tasks
Diversity	Including and respecting a wide range of people, customs, and lifestyles
Education/Wisdom	Gaining knowledge or understanding through formal or experiential learning
Comfort	Having a satisfying and safe existence above what is necessary
Urgency	Speed of delivering a result; pressing necessity
Teamwork	Cooperative effort with people aligned for a single purpose or goal
Justice	The upholding of what is just; fair treatment and due reward with honor, standards, or law
Money/Wealth	An abundance of valuable material possessions or resources; riches
Quality	Having a high degree of excellence or refinement
Relationships	Connection existing between people related to or having dealings with each other
Courage	Mental or moral strength to venture, persevere, and withstand danger, fear, or difficulty
Legacy	Accomplishing goals today with heritage in mind
Authenticity	Being authentic, trustworthy, or genuine
Results	Achieving favorable or concrete outcomes or effects
Humility	Meekness or modesty in behavior, attitude, or spirit; not arrogant or prideful

Impact	Making a strong, positive, and immediate impression on another or others
Equipping Others	Providing what others need, or desiring to help them
Structure	Organized formality in processes or systems
Perfection	Continually striving for the pinnacles of excellence
Logic	Relying on reason to deduce or decide
Recognition	Attention or favorable notice in front of others
Community	A group of people with a common characteristic or interest living together
Customer Focus	Attention to the needs, desires, and satisfaction of clients or customers
Collaboration	To work jointly with others or together, especially in an intellectual endeavor

Now that we've selected our top 20 values from that select group, let's narrow that selection down to only 10 values. And finally, select only 6 values. You may also have another value—for example, joy, hope, or grace—that does not appear here. Please select that as one of your 6.

Why 6, and not 20 or 10? Because selecting 6 values forces us to make tough choices and compartmentalize groups. For example, among our top 10, let's say we have honesty, trust, and integrity, and when we narrow down to 6, 1, 2, or all 3 of these may not survive that round. I've seen people putting family, relationships, and parenting in their top 10, only to have 1 value remaining, the one that is core because it's one of the top 6 values, and we anchor our energy around supporting these 6.

Why is 6 so important? Because with these 6 core values, we will work with people, groups, or companies that support these 6. If we find ourselves in circumstances in which these 6 are not being supported, we will either change the environment to satisfy our values, or we'll leave. That's it. Fix it or leave. Otherwise, if we allow our values to be compromised, we give short shrift to our values, and we know it. And we then become upset, unproductive, or disengaged.

As you share these values with colleagues and family, you may find others have a value (or values) that is not one you selected, and you may be surprised to find that value among their remaining 6 core values. This is rich learning, when you realize someone's core value is one that you discarded, or did not even make your top 20! They have this value in their top 6 core values, and you didn't have it in your top 20. You saw it, and quickly discarded it as, "Well, this isn't me," and you moved on to the next value. People you work with, or family members, have this value as one of their core values—and you dismissed it.

And in the real world we do that, but not by discarding a word on a piece of paper. Rather, we do it with glance at our watch while the other person is talking. Speaks volumes! It is the similarities and differences in our core values that shape our behaviors, which are observed by others. They shape our cultures and define us. The odd word in someone else's selection, the one you didn't choose, is diversity, and how we respect and appreciate that difference defines our culture and ourselves. Words indicating values become very important, particularly as we listen to the stories behind them.

So where do these values come from? They come from our parents, teachers and caregivers as we were growing up. I mean take a look at your top values, and ask yourself, "What did my mom, dad, caregiver, favorite teacher, say to me once forcefully, or over and over again, that I recall?" Think about it. These values shape our decisions and judgments in every way. These values shape our behaviors and collectively these behaviors in a company or team, shape our culture.

One of my top 6 value words is Fun. I recall being in 9th grade, being driven to school by my mom, and as I looked out the window of her car, I saw seniors walking along with girlfriends, letterman jackets, arms full of Calculus books, and plans for college, and some even driving. Man, I was determined to be cool. So as I sat in my mom's Buick, I recall trying to be cool, and talking cool, and acting more like I knew what's going on than my greasy haircut suggested. At the next traffic light on Reading Road, she talked to me. Not normal talk, with her driving. The car was stopped, and she turned her shoulders to me, and said, "Jim, you've got all kinds of time to be old—be a kid as long as you can!" It wasn't a passing comment—it seemed like a decree. I remember the time of year, what she was wearing, the traffic light, some 40 years later. What shapes your values?

Funny: as I recall this story with my mom, she doesn't even remember. I had my 20 year old son do this exercise, and he told me stories of things I'd said to him. I remember the van or the trip, and do not recall my saying some things to him that he said I said. And these comments I can't recall shape his values today.

Lesson: For all the things we plan to say or think we are doing to shape another's behaviors, it is most often in our actions, which we don't plan, take seconds, and mean nothing to us, that last somebody else's lifetime! The power of leadership isn't some heady action, it's the little tiny actions of our inner self coming out for others to observe.

Developing a deeper sense of caring and family as a component of my value system is, in part, what makes me want to be a better person—and a better parent, spouse, son, and brother. If you want to be a better salesperson, be a better person. If you want to be a better leader, believe in who you are!

ADJUSTING TO CHANGE

One of the greatest feats of leadership and adjusting to change was exemplified by Captain Ernest Shackleton, who hoped to be the first to cross Antarctica in 1914. Shackleton, captain of the *Endurance*, and his men were trapped near the South Pole in the harshest of conditions, stranded for months on an ice floe that had crushed their ship. The crew now had a new goal: survival. Shackleton's crew achieved their new goal: all 28 men survived.

As the men got off the stranded ship and discarded unneeded items, one sailor was about to throw out a banjo. Shackleton insisted he keep it, because it might be needed later to lift the men's spirits. Even in such dire circumstances, he was a leader who knew the value of optimism and hope to combat the fear and sadness that soon would threaten to descend on his men. Such fear can lead to paralysis and death.

The Shackleton story is often cited in leadership circles. Shackleton would have made a great project leader. In 1903, he was determined to become the first to reach the South Pole. He was part of Commander Roald Amundsen's failed expedition that year. Then, in 1911, as he got his ship and funding together for his own expedition, he learned that Amundsen had already reached the pole. That's when Shackleton's goal shifted to being the first to cross Antarctica, only to shift once again when the goal became survival. At one point, all the men climbed aboard three lifeboats and sailed five horrifying days on open seas to reach Elephant Island. Shackleton chose five sailors to join him on an 800-mile trip back to South Georgia Isle to retrieve help and supplies. It took them 15 days before they landed amid crashing waves and treacherous rocks, and then they hiked 32 miles over severe mountain ranges to reach help. Shackleton sailed back to Elephant Island and was reunited with the other 23 sailors.

When he selected the five men to go with him on the journey, Shackleton purposely chose one of the men who had challenged his leadership throughout the crisis. He did not want his negative influence disrupting the men left behind at the camp. In other words: keep your friends close and your enemies closer.

Shackleton did everything he could to keep the team and spirit of survival alive. On their journey in the enclosed boat, the five men had very few rations. As the journey lengthened and the sailors needed water, Shackleton would allow them to drink a small amount, insisting they all did so at the same time so they could see the water was being rationed fairly. That action reinforced their common goal of saving their resources. They functioned as a team, with shared goals and a common interest in success.

For all of us, our goals shift when our original plan is no longer workable, or when a new plan emerges, based on new knowledge. Change is all around us. We endure changes in our environment and in our temperaments. Our ability to adapt depends on the degree of change required and whether we are prepared to accept and deal with the challenges.

Before the Civil War, leadership in the United States was more about who you knew. Even battlefield generals and leaders were, in many cases, promoted and appointed to positions based on who they knew in Congress or political leadership roles. West Point changed a lot of that.

Is leadership born or trained? I say yes to both. I became a mom and a dad. I'm not sure I was born or trained for either, and had to do both. Certainly, leadership skills can be trained, and being a really effective leader means more than having all the best skills. Shackleton, whether through training or instinct, built an amazing outcome. Was it a great team? They had struggles as a team, real life-and-death struggles, but in the end they survived. They achieved the greatest and, really, only goal. Whether their survival resulted from instinct or training, the adventure was amazing. Many of our key tenets of successful management and leadership can be learned from this incredible adventure.

GETTING THE RIGHT PEOPLE

Hiring the right people, and fostering the right relationships, we've been led to believe, mean "putting your best foot forward," or, "if you have nothing nice to say, say nothing at all." When Shackleton went about selecting his crew, he posted a sign to attract men interested in joining him. His ad to recruit sailors read: "Men wanted—for hazardous journey. Low wages, bitter cold, long hours of complete darkness. Safe return doubtful. Honour and recognition in event of success." The next day he had 5,000 respondents, for the 28 positions he ultimately filled.

I wonder how many would respond today. Shackleton hired men with experience, and a positive attitude. They were all optimists, and he said later that he hired people "believing character and temperament more important than technical ability."

People want and need a challenge. Some of us even want a death-defying challenge. We want mastery and validation of our skills; we want to beat the odds and achieve. Not all of us, but those who have "competitiveness" as a core value, may be drawn to such a challenge today.

Shackleton has shown us the power and true measure of leadership. While enduring setbacks, a leader still can show others the way to go forward.

Goals shift as life shifts and prepares us for the next step. We learn to trust new beginnings: new bosses, a new spouse, new stepchildren, new fear, new pain, and new forms of success and happiness. We can change our goals. We do not change our character or integrity.

At age 15, Mike Schlappi was shot accidently by a friend who was playing with a gun. Mike would never walk again. He'd had dreams of becoming a professional athlete. Those dreams were gone in one painful instant. Mike went on to earn four wheelchair Olympics medals for the United States. He lives in Salt Lake City, and today he is a model father and husband, and he is a motivational speaker, telling us not to give up the dream.

He proudly says if you can't stand up, then stand out! And in changing times, anchor down around your values and change the things you do each day.

Sometimes perseverance is a matter of knowing when to shift execution or strategy. You don't need to change yourself. Keep being yourself; just change the goal.

"MAN, CAN THIS KID PITCH!"

You've got to know your strengths. Remember the story of the small boy who comes outside with a baseball in one hand and a baseball bat in the other, and he is determined to be the best baseball player in the world. And he throws the ball up in the air, and he picks up his bat, and he swings as hard as he can, and he misses the ball. So he picks up the ball back up and says, "I'm the best baseball player in the world." He throws the ball up in the air and swings again and misses it. And for the third time, he picks the ball up and says, "I'm the best baseball player in the world," and throws the ball in the air and swings through the ball and misses it again. Picking up the baseball, the kid says, "Man, can this kid pitch." Somehow he still has himself convinced he can be the best baseball player in the world. Is he a hitter or a pitcher? You've just got to know your strengths.

STAY TRUE TO YOURSELF

Is success a matter of strategy or execution? Yes. Both. So if you don't achieve desired results, what do you change? Well, you don't change the core values or integrity that defines you and you know to be right. Strategy and execution—we need both, and while we patiently wait for goals to emerge, we keep working on being a better us. Sometimes the goals for our success emerge as we work on our passions and values.

John Maxwell discusses the story of Vonetta Flowers (née Jeffery), which is about a woman who had the talent, strength, and ability to succeed and who had to make a simple goal shift to align strategy and execution. She stayed true to herself.

Vonetta dreamed about being in the Olympics. She learned she had special talent. She achieved a track scholarship to University of Alabama-Birmingham and made strides toward her goal of gaining a spot on the Olympic team. She ended her college career as a seven-time, all-American, competing in the 100-meter and 200-meter sprints, long jump, triple jump, heptathlon, and relays.

Vonetta set her sights on the 1996 Olympics. Unfortunately, she failed to qualify for the team, running slightly behind the leaders. Two days after her second painful failure in the Olympic trials, Vonetta's husband spotted an advertisement for tryouts for the United States Olympic bobsled team. He convinced her to go to the tryouts.

Growing up in the South, Vonetta was not accustomed to cold and snow, and she knew next to nothing about bobsledding. However, at the tryouts her unusual blend of speed and strength proved to be ideal qualities for a brake woman (the person who pushes the bobsled to give it initial momentum and then hops in with the driver). Vonetta was chosen for the team.

Vonetta's decision to join the bobsled team came with a price: two more years of a strict diet, sore muscles, and countless hours dedicated to attaining peak physical fitness. It also meant delaying her dream to be a mom. However, her years of perseverance paid off. Not only did Vonetta achieve her lifelong goal of competing in the Olympics, but she also became the first African American to win a gold medal in the winter Olympics.

THE MEANING OF PERSEVERANCE

Although Vonetta's talent seemed almost limitless, it wouldn't have carried her to the Olympics without an admirable measure of perseverance. Life seems designed to make a person quit. For even the most talented individual, obstacles abound, and failures are commonplace. Only when a person matches talent with perseverance do opportunities become avenues of success.

DETERMINATION, NOT DESTINY

If Vonetta had seen her Olympic dream as a matter of destiny, she likely would have given up after her second failure to make the track and field team. After 17 years of training, the results signaled that her dream wasn't meant to be. She had no logical reason to be hopeful about her prospects. However, she pressed on, determined to find a way to take hold of her goals, and in the end, she was rewarded with success.

STOPPING ONLY WHEN THE TASK IS DONE.

Perseverance doesn't come into play until a person is tired. A year or two after college, Vonetta still was riding the excitement of her collegiate track and field championships. She was young, energetic, and optimistic about the future. Nothing was telling her to stop, and consequently she needed nothing extra to keep going.

However, after a taste of disappointment at the Olympic trials, fatigue and discouragement crept up on Vonetta. The mountain of work in front of her began to look more and more daunting, and her dream began to be a little harder to imagine. Nonetheless, Vonetta persevered. She kept believing, she kept training, and she kept running until she finally caught up with success.

THE IMPORTANCE OF TRUST

In many amazing discussions, I've learned leadership starts when someone asks you who, in your life, has been the greatest leader, or they ask whom you associate with good leadership. And often, that person is someone highly trustworthy.

Trust is the cornerstone and the anchor to our success. How long does it take to establish trust? Well, it may never happen. How long does it take to lose trust? We all know it can be within a matter of seconds. How important is trust? It becomes everything to our success. Leaders don't fail others; they fail themselves because they either lack trust or a character imbued with trust, and that becomes their downfall. We talk about the most important part of business being trust, and yet we spend very little time talking about how to build trust. And, like any other skill, there is a way to build trust.

When you ask people why someone deals with them in business instead of with others, trust is often at the top of the list. Hyler Bracey, in his book *Building Trust*, has a simple formula. He uses TRUST as an acronym.

The "t" in trust stands for "transparency": "Transparency" is when you admit your own failures in order to get other people to listen to you. In the movie *A League of Their Own*, Tom Hanks confronts Geena Davis when she prepares to leave the baseball team. When she decides that baseball just got too hard for her, his says something like, "You can't quit baseball. It's what gets inside of you. It's what lights you up. You will always regret it if you give up baseball." The reason he had the license to go back and say those things is because, just before that, he told her that he had given up the last five years of his baseball career to drinking, and there wasn't anything he wouldn't do to just get back one day of that. Because he admitted his failings, it gave him license not to tell her what to do, not to say she was under contract or that she should do it, but to say, "You need this. This is important for you. I know you so well that I know you will regret this." That's trust building. That's transparency. It gives you more license to have those tough conversations with critical people.

The "r" stands for "reward": Do you reward people and recognize them with praise, or do you just give them feedback? I believe there is a fine line between coaching and criticizing. Marshall Goldsmith has done some great work in his book *What Got You Here, Won't Get You There*, which talks about "feedforward." So often, feedback sounds like the screech of a microphone when it's being tested and fixed. Feedforward is a process that asks, "What is it you'd like to try and get better at? Let's talk to several people—whether it's about organizational skills or listening skills or time management—and each person should have a couple of ideas for how they could help you improve that specific task." Feedforward is conducted with each person saying "thank-you" for the input, with no judgements stated. Our coaching done more as a reward, less correction, requires us to think. "Think" is also an acronym for coaching. Our coaching acronym of T-H-I-N-K, asks is our coaching:

- Timely
- Helpful
- Intuitive
- Necessary
- Kind

The "U" in trust is for "unconditional support": Hyler Bracey had a great perspective considering that over 60 percent of his body had been recently burned and he was not sure if he'd ever be a motivational speaker or author again. He was scheduled to give a presentation but not sure he could do it. His wife helped him get dressed and he flew to the town where he was to give his presentation. He went to his hotel room without dinner and lay in bed in his suit because, having been so badly burned, he couldn't get the suit off. After he spoke the next day to a standing ovation, he rode back to the airport in a cab, recognizing that the only reason he had been able to get up to do that speech was the unconditional support, love, and caring of his grandfather, of his brother, of his family members. When we have people in our lives who care more about us than we care about ourselves, we have one of the cornerstones to trust.

The "s" is for "share": As leaders, when we can admit our failings, let people know what's really going on, and ask for their help, with words such as "I could sure use your help," or "I sure screwed up," that's a powerful way to build trust. In fact, the word help has so many connotations for real leadership and is so critical to trust-building that we mustn't dismiss the word too quickly. When you ask people for help, you're admitting they have more knowledge than you, and you're offering them an opportunity to assist somebody else. The desire to help others is part of human nature. We want to be assistants and coaches and nurses and provide nurturing care for people. It's in our DNA. Admitting that you need help is a powerful way to let people come closer to you to help you, and listen to you, and for you, in turn, to be more honest and candid with them.

And the last "t" stands for "trust smart": Trust can be the "gullible" kind, meaning—as Steven Covey has talked about—you just trust everyone across the board; or it can be the smart kind—"trusting smart"—meaning, "I recognize there are certain things about this individual that allow me to trust this person on this particular issue, but based on past experience, I may not just trust him/her on that other issue, and that's fair." The example would be two former business partners who, after years of mending fences and taking vacations together, consider joining forces again. One partner says, "I'm a great friend and a great partner, and I love you and our vacations with our families, and I would prefer not to do business again because we've learned together that's not our best vehicle for success."

So often we look at success or failure as a result of either strategy or execution—the brains and the hands. Success requires that both go well, yet so often we hear the blame game: Was it strategy that failed, or execution? Brains plan, and hands do, and if the body lacks either, you can be sure that things won't get done. Yet we persist in finding somebody to blame.

Strategy and execution are words of intellect, not of the human heart. Joy, faith, and hope are human words. We need to build character, integrity, and trust.

If strategy and execution were built with trust, they would proceed far better. Trust can build up a team even when it is losing, to rise like a Phoenix to win, or at least to grow.

Some companies and sales organizations, and certainly Wall Street, seem to be less about leadership and more about achievements. Any company can win sales for a quarter, or a year, or a decade. And after all that winning, the next years will require even more. Success requires continued growth and that is best achieved through trust. Involve all stakeholders in both strategy and execution and the result will be a deepening of mutual trust, which stimulates growth and increases exponentially the chances of winning again and again.

I recently had a discussion with a member of the Sales Leadership Alliance (SLA) who described an intradepartmental battle at her company where the sales leadership felt strongly they knew the needs of the customers and salespeople better than the human resources team. The battle lines were drawn, and trust evaporated. Small alliances of strange bedfellows were formed to protect turfs and egos.

How much better it can be when, instead of disputing roles and responsibilities, people see one another as human and appreciate their values! That engenders trust, the basis for communication. We see one another, not as strategists and executors but, rather, as brothers, moms, caregivers, people who matter to somebody. When people can do that, they have a fighting chance to build something unique that transcends the brain-and-hand analogy. Instead, the task becomes more like navigating a river, with everyone's thoughts and effort—their brains and hands—needed if all are to survive and achieve.

BUSINESSES NEED TO GROOM THEIR PEOPLE

In today's world, 85 percent of productivity involves intellectual property, as opposed to 1965 when 85 percent of world productivity was measured in hard goods (DDI research). Today it's brokering, insurance, risk management, portfolio development, banking, and service industry management. In 1965 it was manufacturing of appliances, automobiles, and military controls, farming, manufacturing processes, and line management.

The command-and-control model of management worked effectively in 1965 but fails today, now that people make the difference. "Our people are our greatest asset," big companies like to say, but in today's world, if they don't demonstrate that, they will be living with unmanageable turnover and retention problems.

DEALING WITH A NEW
GENERATION OF WORKERS

Leadership must be redefined in today's rapidly changing world, and it must bridge the generations. "Why anybody thinks they will produce a gazelle by mating two dinosaurs is beyond me," writes Tom Peters, author of *In Search of Excellence*. One might think of the merger of two big pharmaceutical companies, but the absurdity holds true for so much else too as the old ways try to give birth to the new ways, for better or for worse. Most of today's kindergartners will one day hold jobs that do not exist today. We must adjust.

Big used to beat small. Now, fast beats slow. The latest generation thinks and talks differently, with different values. When I meet someone, I might ask: "So, what kind of work are you in?" My kids are far more likely to say, "So, what are you up to?" or "What's going on for you?" They don't even use the word *work* in discussing themselves, or their job, or their career. When I was growing up, I was entertained by TV and movies. In today's high-tech world, it's more about involvement and integration with the world. We participate in games, Wii, texting, tweets, and blogs, and all aspects of entertainment and work are melding. Our pace has quickened.

Recently, a neighbor and I were talking about his colleagues' inability to hire a talented Harvard graduate into his IT company. He offered the prospect a six-figure income, and the kid's response was, "Sorry, man, you're messin' up my powder." My neighbor wondered what that meant. I explained that "powder" is the young man's ski time, which he wasn't going to give up for Monday-morning conference calls or mid-week meetings—not 9 to 5.

The "9-to-5" model may not even exist in 15 years. We face the challenge of getting work done in a world that still marches to the daytime shift. Research shows the new generation thinks and talks in terms of work, learning, and fun being one big activity. Their parents grew up getting the best grades, getting into the best college, getting the best job, making the most amount of money in the shortest period of time, to retire as early as possible—and only then have fun. Not so for today's generation.

What value do we provide to our employees? I have challenged my trainers over the years to consider this: "What do you believe the people you train here would pay, from their own pocket, to come to your training session: $5, $100, $1000, or $5,000? How much real value do we provide?

If you take care of your employees, hotel magnate Bill Marriott advised, they'll take care of your customers. What do we do to value our employees? The best chance to manage the generation gap is to genuinely understand the motivations of younger employees and offer praise and encouragement. If we don't appeal to what they truly value, the gap will widen. We must pay attention to what they tell others we are doing, despite how much we think we are doing.

Chapter 6

RIIIIIIIGHT!!!!

"Sign, sign, everywhere sign
Blockin' out the scenery, breakin' my mind.
Do this, don't do that, can't you read the sign?"

—Five Man Electrical Band, "Signs," 1970

T he word came on the day after Abraham Lincoln's inauguration: Fort Sumter was short on supplies and would be forced to surrender to the Confederates unless troop reinforcements came soon.

Lincoln's responded brilliantly. If he did nothing to support the fort, he would be seen as weak in the North. If he sent troops, he would be seen as the aggressor responsible for firing the first shots of the Civil War. Lincoln therefore sent word that he would supply the fort but not reinforce it with troops unless the fort was attacked. The Confederates faced a dilemma: If they allowed the resupply, the secession would lose its credibility. If they attacked first, they would become the aggressor and reward Lincoln with a rallying cry for the North.

The Confederacy soon began the bombardment. The Southern leaders, unwilling to back down, were determined to be right. Lincoln had not operated out of ego or controlled the outcome. He had simply issued a clear communication that established clear consequences for actions taken.

OUR BURNING DESIRE NOT TO BE WRONG

Think about how we tirelessly work on a project to have every single dot line up just right. Then we can say, "Look! I did it perfectly, so don't blame me if anything is wrong. I should be congratulated!"

We have this burning desire not to be wrong, and in our determination to gain acceptance we sometimes do silly things. Many of us have experienced occasions when a friend or client seemed to be overly agitated about something we thought was trivial. People get so involved in the rightness of their position and can't seem to let go of the issue. Our brains focus on the "fight or flight" response, on the external threat, and less on good decision making and judgment.

There was a scene on the TV show *Malcolm in the Middle* about an encounter between two drivers in a parking lot. One bumps his car door into the other's car while removing a package. "The least you can do is say you're sorry!" the offended driver says. He is making his position clear, drawing the proverbial line in the sand. He then opens his door to bump the other car, yelling, "Well, it's not like I did any damage." And thus begins an argument with both drivers smashing their doors back and forth into each other's cars and yelling at the top of their lungs.

Such childish behavior reflects a primal desire to not look wrong. Marshall Goldsmith tells of two monks strolling beside a stream and stopping to meditate. They hear from across the stream the cries of a young woman struggling to cross the rushing water. The monks talk about the fact that they are not allowed to soil their clothes and touch a woman, even if she needs help. The first monk ignores these concerns and goes over to help the woman and carry her across the stream. When he returns, the other monk lectures and scolds him for his action, reminds him again later that day that he behaved improperly, and feels so irritated he cannot sleep. He even awakes the "transgressor" that night to further admonish him. Looking at his accuser, the first monk says, "I only carried her across the water. You have carried her all the way back here. And you still carry her in your inability to sleep."

"MY BAD..."

"No, that's not right," we insist. "No, you misunderstood me!" We blame the other for not getting our point. That's like blaming the customer for not buying. It's as if we were saying, "Silly customers. How dumb they are. They didn't even buy my clearly, factually stated points. Oh, well: their loss!" And we've lost the chance to find a friend, build an ally, learn something, or look even more *powerful* to others by saying, "My bad."

Yes, there is real power in saying we're sorry. To admit our mistake is to elevate our humanness, and that's more powerful than title, money, or fame. Powerful, in terms of influence and even more importantly in making ourselves feel good. We all have apologized and walked away feeling better. We get it off our plate so that we can move forward, instead of overthinking a past issue and trying to deal with things we can't control anyway.

I love to see the response that athletes often make after they screw up a big play. Their teammates scowl and stare at them as they make a horrible fumble, or bad pass. And the player at fault simply mouths the words, "My bad." In a simple, single action, all is understood, and the team can move forward to make corrections. When you know the others are aware of their mistake, here's a novel approach you can take: Stop correcting. Just nod, say thanks, and smile.

Writing this book was not my strength. I work with small and large teams in coaching and leadership situations. As I started and stopped this book over the years, I found myself simply wanting this to be over and done with. This kind of writing isn't something I have done often. My editor gave me updates and suggestions. Still, I found myself behind on timelines and unsure what messages were resonating with the reader. In a moment of frustration, I sent a note to him and his team saying that I was disappointed in his efforts and felt the project had stalled. I realized the next day that I was the one behind on my commitments, and that I was disappointed in myself and had taken it out on him. When I called him later, we clarified our positions. "Jim," he said, "this should be fun, not a chore. Just find and take the time to relax with this, and we'll have a fine product." I felt better. So did he, and I could move forward without harboring an undiscussed feeling. It's that harboring that leads to thoughts and words that should simply be in the past. Let go, man!

CLARITY FIRST

In the movie *Meatballs*, Bill Murray plays a camp counselor who is trying to motivate summer camp kids to win against the Mohawks in a summer camp Olympics. His campfire message is: "It just doesn't matter." His energy, passion, and cheering motivate the kids to win. Though the message isn't "right," it is clear. Relax, do your best, and with a sense of exhilarating fun—that's winning.

After 9/11, when then Mayor Rudy Giuliani was talking to reporters about how many people died that horrible day, he might have been "right" if he had spoken about the loss of nearly 3,000 innocent souls. He chose, however, to say something clear, simple, and motivating: one loss was one too many. That's leadership: taking the complex, and making it simple and clear. It motivates and inspires, and that's what's right.

We reason through logic, and we are motivated through emotion. Emotions aren't right or wrong; they are feelings. How much better if we could just be clear and give people the basic information they need to reach solutions! That way they can do their work and move forward, correcting their course as they learn. It's more important to be clear than to be right.

Clarity also means knowing when to follow a rule. Suppose the posted signs on a lake read, "No swimming," and as you pass the lake, you see a child struggling in the middle of the lake. You dive in and help the struggling swimmer to safety. You broke the "no swimming" rule. Sometimes, to honor a higher goal means not following every rule. The rule was established for safety, and in this case the proper response to safety was to break that rule. One must keep in mind why the rule exists, not just follow it blindly.

In business communications, clarity should be the emphasis if we expect the support of other departments and a sense of collaboration. If we expect a sales department to execute a certain instruction, why is the marketing department changing the communication at the eleventh hour? To say they are right? Today's communications often see change by the hour. The teams that are expected to execute those changes may find out about them minutes before they are to act. Everybody possesses lots of knowledge. Our best chance of success is to harness, guide, and nurture that collective knowledge in messages focused on clarity, not a determination to be correct.

GANDHI'S SYMPHONY OF CLARITY

In the mid-1950s, Ghandi was fighting for India's freedom from Britain. He was not an elected official. He wasn't a delegate to any political or parliamentary group. He was just one individual, determined to gain his freedom.

On one occasion, Ghandi addressed a mob of Indian leaders who were angry because of British oppression. Ghandi was not about violence. When we want to win our point with anyone, to simply yell it seems to do no good. Rather, dialogue, listening, and questions asked to acquire knowledge, not to challenge, gained him an audience. And he supported his countrymen's frustrations. "I am prepared to die for freedom," he said, and as the room went quiet, he added, "and I will never kill for it." Ghandi knew that killing was wrong, and that he would never sway world opinion, which he needed, if he supported immoral and inhuman acts.

Ghandi was powerful because he sought peaceful means to produce change—fierce on the issue, easy on the people.

On another occasion he spoke to the British parliament and was allowed to present his case for freedom as he had attracted a great deal of attention on this issue. Ghandi spoke convincingly and passionately about his desire for India to be free of British rule. Some representatives of the media were allowed to cover the event. A British journalist asked the Indian journalist sitting next to him how it was that Ghandi could speak nonstop for over two hours without a single note. The Indian journalist reportedly said, "Ghandi has only one speech. For everybody. He has the same message for his people, the media, his family, the British." Everyone knew Ghandi's message. He lived congruence. He did not have one message for his people, one for political leaders, and another for friends. He never had to manage two stories. His clarity is called congruence. His thoughts, feelings, and actions, were a symphony of clarity.

C'MON, RIGHT IS RIGHT!

We have been indoctrinated with the belief that getting it right is of supreme importance. In school we hope to be right on tests so that we can get good grades and go to the right college and land the right job to provide the right living for our family. We do the right thing to get more of what we want, whether it's praise, or money, or a promotion. We seek more control of our lives and others' lives. By being right and making the right decisions, we get to control others. What a goal!

So much of our quest to be right stems from what Mom and Dad repeatedly told us: "Don't go out in the rain without your galoshes or you'll catch cold. Always wait half an hour after eating before swimming, or you'll get cramps, fold up like a cheap lawn chair, and drown!" Much of what we have heard is about the right way to keep safe, and much of it is myth. Yet the words have become part of our belief systems. Hundreds of sayings guide our thinking, and our doing, as we strive to do right.

Sadly, when we are in a position to lead people, we apply these same key principles, hoping for better living and safety. We play it safe, and some call that leadership. After all, we didn't spend all those years in school just to be wrong and go against the rules, right? Being right starts early. Parents, determined to be right, choose issues of safety as their platform. It's always safety first.

It can therefore be scary when being a truly successful leader means not being right but being, in fact, able to admit you are wrong and not taking the safe course. To be safe is like everything else we do. It is designed to look right and safely protect our ego. We want to save face with others and show that we aren't wrong. The unsafe thing to do is to care more about higher responsibilities than about our own egos, to care about other people's feelings and engagement more than about our own success.

LEADERS NEED HUMILITY

As Ken Blanchard puts it: "People with humility don't think less of themselves; they just think of themselves less." Or in the words of rocker Jim Morrison: "When you make peace with authority, you become authority."

THE "RIGHT" STUFF

Too many leaders are overly concerned about being right. We need to be right. We were raised to be right. We got to positions of leadership because we were right—about finances, risks, acquisitions, promotions, business decisions. So we have evidence to support our belief that being right is important. Is it the most important thing?

Would you rather report to a leader who is always right or one who admits he/she is not right, and who, in fact, actively admits, "Sorry. I am wrong about this." I once asked a management candidate this question during an interview: "After a year as a manager, would you want your people to say, 'Man, my boss sure knows a lot!' or 'Man, my boss sure understands me'?"

We're so programmed to be right that we miss the chance to truly be successful as coaches, and that success calls for us to set a clear direction, not to be correct about every detail. It's the sense that our boss genuinely cares about us that matters, and only the boss can deliver that value.

CONTROL VS. COLLABORATION

In the twentieth century leadership indeed was all about being right. It was the command and control generation. It was about time clocks, labor forces, military leadership, and rigorous discipline. One of the good things to come from that era was a sense of leadership as grown from "followership." If the golden rule is, "Do unto others as you would have others do unto you," the rule of great leadership is "Do unto others as if they were me." It is about maximizing our power not through what we know but, rather, what we ask. We don't like to be told, and we love to be asked. Followers know how to get in line, and they know whom to follow in line. Leaders who aren't good followers are less experienced at humility and admitting mistakes.

As Goldsmith says, "What got you here won't get you there!" The "there" is the twenty-first century and the need to perform at a higher level each year. We want growth in our business, personal knowledge, and capability. The twenty-first century is the era of knowledge and intellectual property. Organizations and people talk in terms of collaboration, team, alignment, balance of life, and personal values. The command-and-control model does not work for people today.

I was in a discussion recently with my neighbor, an older gentleman, about the "younger generation." We shared how they seem determined to have their own way. He grew up in the world of command and control. His bosses were former military personnel and baby-boomer, time-clock, manufacturing-era leaders. They could be harsh and fierce with expectations for productivity. He believed the younger generation didn't appreciate the hard work and almost "hell-week" mentality that went into being successful. We debated whether these Gen Y and millennial workers were, in fact, adhering to their values, refusing to be bullied by corporations. Although he grew up feeling the same way, his generation was not empowered to communicate those feelings to leaders. Today there is a war on talent, not labor. Top graduates of universities are not accepting the command-and-control methods of a manufacturing-era leader. The millennials are saying what the baby boomers could not: "I'm not going to lead a life inside a corporate world that demands I get the best grades, the highest-paying job, the most money, and retirement at the earliest age." The millennials are tying fun, work, and learning into how they behave, and less 9 to 5.

The collaborative approach can work well in customer relationships. Nobody wants to be handled. To sell, we were told to uncover the objections, find out the concerns, dig deeper. As the customers talk, they try to reinforce their argument, and our job is to get them talking about the positive aspects of our product or service. We learn from 80 percent of what we say and 20 percent of what we hear.

Our customers talk and try to convince themselves and us of their argument. If they speak well of us, we are to say to them, "That's interesting. Tell me more." If they speak badly of us, we say, "Thank you," and move to another topic. Likewise, if they speak well of the competition. However, if they speak badly of the competition, you should again say, "Thanks. Tell me more." By getting the customer to talk positively about you, your product or service, you benefit from them teaching themselves about your product or service.

A BOSS WHO ISN'T BOSSY

A true leader, however, is like the front wheels of a car, steering forward. The managers and supervisors are like the rear wheels, keeping things moving along. When asked what makes the best manager, the most common response is this: "The one who leaves me alone." In business, if you want success with your teams, you can lead for growth or control—not both.

People have no interest in being controlled—none! We are creatures of knowledge, intellect, emotions, and choices. "You're not my boss!" we say. And it's true: No boss really controls anyone. Supervisors and managers are responsible for workers in certain jobs achieving certain goals. They manage your job description and the goals. They do not own you. If you left the company, they would have no say about your time or activity. You can control things, not people.

We consider bosses to be leaders only when they realize that they don't own you and engage you instead—that is, when the boss isn't bossy. It's an interesting word. It can carry negative connotations, evoking images of crime bosses or crooked politicians (Boss Tweed) who were seen as command-and-control people, not empathic miners of human potential.

I have done experiments in which I assigned leaders to work with teams to create structures with building blocks. Beforehand, I told the assigned leaders to either be vacant or to be overly controlling during the exercise. Then the teams set out to build the tallest structure. I found that in terms of getting results, the bad leaders did well. A manager can make things happen for the short term if the role is corrective action, and yet it is a style that doesn't embrace change for the long term. Trying to control people doesn't bring out their best.

HONEST OR RUDE?

I coached a manager years ago who had two team members who did not get along. They would feud and quibble over the most minor of issues. The concern was that one of the quibblers was the other's supervisor. As the supervisor, she had the greater responsibility for her poor conduct. She was damaging the relationship with her employee, who, incidentally, was a top performer.

This went on for several weeks. I suggested that the manager talk to that supervisor. The supervisor's response to him was: "Hey, I'm just being honest." He didn't disagree. Instead, he told her, "And *you* are being rude!" Two perspectives on the same situation. Although she was right, she was not clear about her role as leader, which was to listen respectfully and find a creative resolution, not push her rightness or be bossy.

PRAISE OTHERS, BLAME YOURSELF FIRST—AND LEARN

I never said it was easy. There can be a price to pay when we are leaders. In *Winning with People*, John Maxwell states that the greater your leadership role, the more rights you give up. You sacrifice the right to complain and blame in exchange for accepting more responsibility for the outcome. And when the outcome is good, your responsibility is to congratulate and praise others, not yourself. When the outcome is bad, you accept full responsibility for the shortfall. In the long term, the setback may be your greatest instruction, which leads to future success. That's also your job as a leader: to find the greatest instruction for the next possible success.

Be prepared. People will say that you "just don't get it." What they should realize is that they are the ones who don't get you. We can be so adamant about our rightness that when we perceive that others disagree with us, we immediately size up their behaviors and try to assess whether they are against us. That's how important being right becomes. We believe our rightness. We instruct others on our rightness about selling or training or marketing. If they agree with us, great, and if they don't, well, they don't get it. And more importantly if we perceive they agree or disagree, we immediately size up their behaviors to assess if they are with us or against us.

TO BE RIGHT SHOULDN'T BE A MISSION

I'm not advocating we should be less right. However, we should not be demanding personal credit for being right. If we were less interested in establishing who was right and who's to blame, we could provide more of a sense of support for others and help a project move ahead more smoothly. Frankly, those who share the limelight have the better chance for stronger relationships and greater value in their leadership. Real leadership is based on trusting relationships, and that provides the power for great results.

It seems as if we are wired to believe there is an "economy of rightness." If we give too much credit to someone else, there won't be enough left for us. Real leadership gains momentum and power from giving credit to others, just as leaders gain joy and hope when they give those qualities to others. Over the years I've seen managers and business people ask for input or feedback. These are some of their responses to what they hear:

- "Yeah, I thought of that."

- "I told them what to do, but they didn't ..."

- "Sure I was going to do that, but here's why ..."

- "I could have done that, but chose not to."

- "I've already done that."

And the list goes on. We don't fully acknowledge or allow the feedback for fear that we will be perceived as not having been right or smart enough to have thought about those ideas first. In school we measured rightness through tests. In today's business we measure rightness socially, through communication, and in how we build relationships. It comes down to our ability to convince somebody of our rightness. We do this at home, with friends, and at work: "I'd better show I was right first because that's where the reward is." We do it as fast talkers, or loud talkers, with our hand in the air, or with loads of data and evidence.

LEADERS VALUE OTHERS' INPUT

Real leadership is letting go of that premise of correctness. Yes, it's hard to do. Everything we've been taught is about looking right ourselves, not about showing others they are right. Relationship and leadership power comes from valuing the collective inputs of others. In a recent *Harvard Business Review* article, psychologist John Gottman stated that the best way to build strong relationships is to sprinkle them with an imaginary salt shaker of yeses. That means regularly making positive, affirmative statements:

- "Sure. You bet.
- "That sounds great!
- "Great! Thanks for the feedback.
- "Sure seems like a good idea.
- "Keep up the great comments.
- "Very helpful—good for you.
- "That must make you feel good."

HOW WE JUDGE

Through it all, through those decisions that we make or don't make, we begin to evaluate other people—those on our teams or those around us. We judge others on their actions, and we judge ourselves on our intentions.

Let's say I'm driving home from work and my wife calls. "Honey, will you pick up the laundry?" And I say, "Sure." Then about a half an hour later I walk through the front door with no laundry, and she says, "Honey, did you get the laundry?" And I say, "No."

What goes through her mind? What is she saying to herself about me? Yeah, you got it: "You don't listen. You don't care. It's all about you. You don't seem to think that my concerns are very important," and the list goes on. She has already judged my actions. Here is what I might be saying to myself when I walk through that door with no laundry: "I came home a different way," or "I have to go out and pick up the kids at soccer practice, so I'll just do it then," or "I went by the laundry but it was locked," or "The road construction in front of that laundry was bad," or "I was out buying flowers for your mother." Whatever it may have been, I've still judged myself on my intentions, not on my actions, and we judge others on their actions.

If somebody cuts you off in traffic, you might feel angry. However, if you considered that the driver might be a mother on the way to the hospital because her son had just been hit by a car, you might back up and say, "It's okay. You go right ahead." We judge others on their actions because they've cut us off, in one way or another. We don't consider that they might have a higher priority than ours.

HOW WILL YOU BE JUDGED AS A BOSS?

Ever see someone leave the office building at 3 p.m. with briefcase and car keys in hand, obviously going home early from work? "Now, there's a slacker," you might think. "Not committed. Lazy." If the situation is reversed, and it's you who is going home at 3 p.m., you tell yourself, "Well, I'm traveling all weekend," and "I can take care of things on my BlackBerry and through e-mails. No big deal."

Which perception will gain our greatest amount of time, commitment, and engagement? In order to elicit statements from our team members describing us as understanding and not simply a know-it-all, we need to let go of being so concerned with being or looking right. Stop worrying about whether others "just don't get it." If anything, we are the one they don't get. For leaders, it's less about what we say or even do, but rather knowing that others will remember how we make them feel. We have to listen and question more, versus tell more. We need to respect the opinions of others. In the words of Dr. Wayne Dwyer: "In the battle to be right or kind, choose kind; it's closer to your values and the values of others."

Chapter 7

SUCCESS AND WINNING REDEFINED

"Success is going from failure to failure without loss of enthusiasm."
—Winston Churchill

*"We are all born with only two fears: the fear of
falling and noise. All other fears are learned."*
—Claire-Muriel Maslen, *Psychology Today*

I once asked my dad how much money he made. He said, "Why do you want to know?"

"I just wanted to know," I said. Actually, I had observed that my friend's dad had just bought a new car and I wondered why we didn't buy one.

"Jim, we have enough to take care of your sister and you, and even support both your educations through college," my father said.

"So how much do you make so you can do all of that?" I asked. I thought I was so clever.

"You don't need to know," he told me. "I wouldn't want you to start defining the people around you that way." He knew that as a child I might grade my dad versus other dads and make value decisions such as who the better dad was.

My dad never did tell me how much money he made, and I never found out. I remembered his words and practiced the same philosophy with my own kids, and I believe that has served them well.

EMPTY CHATTER ABOUT SALARIES

The Internet is filled with the chatter of people who feel they are underpaid and who quote exact salaries and bonuses. As I read these pages of comments, I am struck by how much negative energy goes into all these conversations. I have asked business people why they are so curious about other people's income. "I want to know what I'm worth on the open market or at another company," they reply, or "I think I should be paid more than other people," and they proceed to give some reason, or play some blame game. Their comments sound victim-like. When I ask how they feel about such discussions, they usually say they don't like them. It seems they feel people are less than honest about their income as they try to look like winners. Vegas, after all, wasn't built on the gamblers who won; it was built on gamblers who lost and told others they won.

Discussions around money are easily manipulated. Vacation time, benefit packages, relocation policies all influence income and compensation and aren't often detailed when people talk about compensation in round numbers. And I know from coaching employees and managers that leaving a company for a few thousand dollars more in promised compensation doesn't lead to greater happiness, success, or achievement of career goals over time.

It's a mean cycle—and is that winning? In measuring whether we are winners, we emphasize the wrong values. Some people come to believe that it's lonely at the top yet they strive to get there faster than the next guy. For every winner, there is a loser, they believe, and our experiences reinforce that thinking. People seem to believe there is an economy of winning: if you aren't winning, you are losing. And so, we strive to look and talk like winners, and say things such as, "There is no such thing as a good loser." What I wish to emphasize is that one of the greatest traits to me in leadership and personal success is to admit we are wrong. By doing so, we more closely align ourselves to others as humans and less as experts, and that, in the end, gives us greater influence.

WINNING IS MORE THAN POWER AND INCOME

If you are like so many people, you feel you are supposed to climb the corporate ladder and achieve: get the best grades, go to the best schools, make the most money, and keep driving to the top of the heap. All along the way, you feel more empowered and more in charge. You are able to talk about other people and make decisions about them, including how much money they will make, whether they will be promoted, their value in society.

Winning in today's society is often measured in income. I can recall looking for ways to better value a sales force. I measured success by how much money the sales force brought in. We have metrics centered on dollars, market share, and year-on-year growth. I remember asking a consultant friend of mine, "How do you measure your success versus other consultants?" His answer: "W-2." He compared his own income on a payroll stub with that of the other consultant. Success was and is measured by the dollars achieved on the income side of the ledger sheet.

And yet we all know of struggling marriages in which the husband or wife is confused. After all, they have been good "providers," haven't they? They makes a luxurious living for their family, and aren't they doing remarkably well? And they wonder why the marriage is dying. They are is slowly learning a lesson: winning is more than the dollars on that ledger sheet.

MONEY CANNOT BE THE TRUE MOTIVATOR

Daniel Pink has done some great work on money and motivation. And for so many corporations where money is believed to be a motivator, the research, more often than not, shows that money is merely a satisfier. When you receive that money, after two weeks, all you've done is pay the Visa bill and other obligations. You believe you should have had more money, and you know in the back of your mind that that money is being used to manipulate your behavior, either through the fear of penalty—not getting money—or the hope of reward—getting more money.

That manipulative process indicates the best that money can do is to become a satisfier. If you truly want to motivate people, praise and recognize individuals, their key values, and their specific activities, all of which tie back to organizational goals.

As we shape this discussion on leadership, based on the changed behaviors and improved attitudes we have talked about, we must consider how others will perceive us. I've asked people in many group presentations I've given, "Who here is in sales?" Only when I ask that question three or four times do most hands in the room go up. People come to realize that the way they dress, the way they talk, and the way they approach other people have to do with the way they create their own brand. They are, in a real way, selling who they are. Whether they are individuals of high quality, or fun, or relaxed, they project other people's perceptions of them.

I've done a lot of work with salespeople because oftentimes they get either a bad rap, or a correct rap, depending on the public's viewpoint. I will tell you this about sales: no one ever came home from a shopping trip and said, "Hey, look at all this stuff somebody sold me." Our job as salespeople, at home or at work, is to create buyers and spend less time pushing our ideas. If you want to be a better salesperson, be a better person.

RELATIONSHIPS THE KEY TO WINNING

There's a story about a study on who could build the best boat: engineers, researchers, or salespeople. Each group was given the same materials and told to do its best to build a boat to cross a big lake. The engineers built one with so many bells and whistles that it sank. As the researchers were putting their boat together, they ran out of time and never actually got it launched. As for the salespeople, they sold all the materials and had a beach party. What you want to get done will depend on whether you are the engineer type, the research type, or the salesperson type.

There are several different influences that can lead to success in selling. The top three influences, in a recent study by Charlie Brennan, were found to be the success that you would have in using the product, your relationship to the buyer, and the quality of the product. Which of those three was number one? Thirty-eight percent of the time, relationships were the most important influence. Think about the relationships in your life that shape your decisions on where to buy a product or service. Your mechanic, your gardener, your pool person, and the one who cuts your hair may not be the best in terms of educational accomplishments. Still, you trust them, and you believe them to offer the best service for you, and that concept of trust becomes the basis for success as we go forward with whatever we do in management and leadership.

Sellers need to look more like personal trainers who challenge the buyer and don't just serve up more of "How can I help?" and "What else can I do for you?" We only continue to talk to sellers when they are interesting and capable of teaching us something. Through thoughtful dialogue and debate, we learn ways to achieve our goals, and customers buy. That forges a better relationship than one merely based on friendliness or neighborliness.

DEFINING REAL SUCCESS

How do your best skills and behaviors define you and your brand? Do all your efforts spell success, or does it look as if you are selling success? What matters most, your knowledge, or your character, or your capacity to help others? Are you somebody's role model?

Here's how our senior sales executives defined success in a recent executive sales summit development meeting here in Irvine:

Someone successful

- sees the bigger picture and focuses on the end result or goal;

- melds effectively with all types of personalities;

- figures out what needs to get done and it gets done!

- refuses to accept no as the answer;

- is consultative and a practice partner;

- has good work ethic;

- is interested in constant education—doesn't just sit back;

- is self-reflective and introspective.

THE HUMAN FLY

Several years ago many people showed up in a large downtown city to see the Human Fly. This man was called that because he could scale buildings straight up the side to the very top.

As the crowd gathered on this particular day, the Human Fly began his climb, and he made great progress in climbing this skyscraper. As he neared the top, he began to struggle as he reached for what he thought was a small ledge protruding from the building. He grabbed it for support but misjudged the object and could not gain leverage to prevent him from falling to his death. Still in his hand was the only thing he had managed to reach: a spider web. Under pressure, sometimes we see things that aren't there or hope for things that are beyond our grasp. We commit ourselves to action and hope for the best, and we may be oblivious to the true risks until it's too late.

Pressured by the crowd to keep climbing, the Human Fly made a fatal mistake. We too are pressured by the crowds, and hopefully we don't lose the solid grip that keeps us safe and sound. To be truly successful, after all, one must be fully grounded in our character and core values, even while reaching for new heights.

A LESSON IN BROADCASTING

It seems so much more important to simply be better, not perfect or always right. There's an old joke: "I knew I had married Ms. Right. I just didn't realize her first name was Always!" Long ago I had an experience in broadcasting that puts so much of our applied learning into focus.

I had the opportunity to be a play-by-play broadcaster for men's basketball at UC Irvine. I was selected to do a home game and was learning to do basketball announcing. I had never played collegiate or professional basketball and had much to learn about fundamentals, such as the rules of one-and-one free throws, and team foul count.

When I was selected to announce a local home game, I met with the everyday play-by-play announcer to review my role and process. I met the head coach and a couple of players, and man, I was set. This was going to be great. As with any new role we strive to take on, or new relationship that seems exciting, we start off eagerly. I didn't know a lot and had much to learn, and the whole thing was exciting.

So, I was handed a series of rules manuals, player profiles, and information on the opposing team, New Mexico State, the coach, players, and statistics. And I began studying. And some of these Eastern Bloc names, such as Chernoskoich, Stycerkoch, and Miesermich, I had to pronounce on the air, and I knew their families and friends would be listening. Their statistics were very impressive, in shooting, assists, blocks, and rebounds. Should I refer to those statistics while announcing? Should I talk only sometimes or just when I was asked a question?

As with our roles at home and work, we have expectations when we go into a new situation, and we often become overwhelmed and frustrated with how much work and learning is associated with our success. Many have abandoned their piano lessons or foreign language studies, even after a significant commitment of time. It becomes just too much and devoid of enjoyment.

As I prepared for game day, I practiced with the announcer and statistician and interviewed players and coaches. After the first half, I began to settle into a routine of what to say and when. Our team slam-dunked, and I chimed in with a "Biggity bam! It's all in!" At least I had fun. And I was gaining confidence and competence as I learned.

I had opportunities to do another game and even go on the road. Although I had learned a great deal and seen some success, I had to consider whether this was a good new direction for my career. I decided to do more traditional business coaching. I applied my experience and learning to other ventures, but the broadcasting experience led me to feel more capable. That was the ultimate achievement of my foray into broadcasting.

Each of us at some time, probably many times, has gone through an experience that began with excitement and then led to some degree of anxiety, fear, and frustration. That is the nature of learning. Our chance to learn and grow comes from taking inventory of our strengths and opportunities and where we can best apply our greatest values.

Chapter 8

HEALTHY COMMUNICATION

"The most powerful word is the silence of a well-timed pause."

—Mark Twain

I t was the first inning of the first game of the 2004 World Series, with the Boston Red Sox playing the Saint Louis Cardinals. Jeff Suppan, pitcher for the Cardinals, found himself to be a runner on third base, a place where pitchers rarely wind up, with a chance to score the very first run of the series.

The next batter hit the ball toward second base and was easily tagged out at first. Meanwhile, the third-base coach yelled "Go! Go! Go!" to Suppan. On the video, we see Suppan start to head for home plate and then, oddly, retreat to third, and when he finally races back for home he is out at the plate. The inning is over.

Later, the third-base coach speculated that perhaps Suppan had heard his words as "No! No! No!" If that was the case, one letter had had a huge impact. It had caused Jeff to hesitate, unsure of his decision. The Cardinals lost that game, as well as the next four games in a sweep by the Red Sox.

Communication is not easy. In fact, it can be exceedingly difficult. We need to go beyond just the words and consider the ways that we express them. How often do we feel that we were clear, appropriate, determined, and urgent, and still find ourselves wondering why no one is listening?

LEADERSHIP BEGINS WITH COMMUNICATION

What do we enjoy most about our jobs? It may not be the work so much as the workplace, the environment where we do our work. Is it a shop? A retail outlet? An office? Windows or cubicle? What do we like best about our workplace or environment?

I can tell you what we value the most: that someone knows our name. Communication begins with knowing names. And when someone gets a nice award for effort and the boss mispronounces or misspells that person's name, everything else that is said or done loses meaning. If leaders want to build trust, which is their greatest job, they should know the names of those they lead!

I still smile to think of a story I once heard about a mailing error. The screw-up occurred at an automated mailing company that sent letters to the mailing list of the archdiocese of a major city. All the mailings were addressed to "Dear Mr. Sister," an absurd mis-communication and just one of many these days when supervisors and employees and friends text and e-mail in what amounts to hieroglyphics.

Several years ago I had an experience that gave me an insight into communication. An African American colleague and I were in Detroit on business, and as we walked into the office where we had an appointment, we saw an older African American woman who was quite agitated. She was yelling—and I mean yelling—at a young Caucasian staffer. My colleague and I excused ourselves, planning to call back at another time.

Back in the car, my friend turned to me in disgust and said, "Man, that crazy lady just set my whole race back another large step!" Seeing that I was puzzled, he explained, "Jim, when people see a white person upset and acting crazy, they just see a crazy person. But when they see a black person upset, they see a black person acting crazy. That kind of behavior shapes people's opinions about my race and about me. That's why I'm annoyed. All my efforts to be professional, and I'm still seen as a professional black guy!" Wow! Welcome to education. I learned so much that day, 25 years ago, and I still recall the moment as if it were yesterday. Sometimes learning isn't in the repetition; it's in the shock of the event, which lodges it into our memory. I will never forget 9/11, for example, and it wasn't the endless replay of the footage that drilled it into me.

Our communication with one another is very confusing. We can't ever seem to get it right. Remember the high school dance, with boys on one side of the hall and girls on the other? Seemed like the other gender was a separate species, and we couldn't talk, just snicker and laugh. Finally, boredom set in, and rejection seemed, well, at least not boring.

Today we move not from one activity to another, but, rather, we conduct several activities all at once. We can watch TV, type on the computer, talk to our mom, answer our cell phone, and drink a cup of coffee at the same time. If only we could add driving while doing all the above, we would be on to something.

As we lead ourselves through daily circumstances, we have an opportunity to also lead others. The essence of great leadership begins with great communication. And that means communicating with other people, not at them. Many people think communication is talking. Actually, it may very well be pausing as you think about the proper answers, and listening to understand the other person.

MORE THAN WORDS

We can persuade other people through reason, and we truly motivate them through emotions. I've often said that we get out of something whatever we put into it. I've told my teenage son that for years.

How we influence people has a lot to do with the way we understand their motivations. As Steven Covey has said, "People don't care what you know until they know how much you care." Influence starts with the things that we say, or the things that people think we say.

Dr. Albert Mehrabian at UCLA did a benchmark study in 1978 on leadership and influence and the ways that we communicate, and it came down to three key influences: our words, our verbal tone, and our nonverbal or body language, totaling 100 percent. It turned out that words only had a 7 percent influence. Verbal skills, tone, pace, and loudness of voice had a 38 percent influence, and influence of nonverbals was as high as 55 percent.

These signals of nonverbal communication—if you look at your watch too fast or too often, if you stand too close or too far away from somebody, if you roll your eyes—speak volumes. All the slideshows you put together, with all those magnificent words, mean nothing if people don't believe through your body language that you genuinely care or that you genuinely have knowledge or confidence in what you're doing.

Body language is crucial to our communication. And today we are connected not only via phone lines, mail routes, zip codes, and area codes. We instantaneously move from an electronic beep to a vibrating tone. We communicate less with our voices and more with keystrokes. We are losing our sense of community and interactivity. We are not communicating; we are connecting. Big difference. Since most of us have personal or professional relationships in which how we feel is more important than what is being said to us, we may be missing big chunks of vital information.

THE WORDS THAT WORK

The six most expensive words may be "We've always done it that way." The three most powerful words are "Act as if ..." John Maxwell explains that you should act as if the person you're doing business with is going to become your boss or become the best salesperson of the year or the community leader that you will admire in the future. If you treat people as if they have those capabilities, what an amazing difference your smile and your body language can make to those communications!

In leadership, the six most important words are: "I totally admit I was wrong." The five most important words are: "You did a great job." The four most important words are: "What do you think?" The three most important words are: "Could you please ...?" The two most important words are: "Thank you." The most important word is: "We." The most unimportant word is: "I."

That's the lineup of leadership words that are on a poster in the office of Bill Marriott, the hotelier who asserted that "employees are no. 1; customers are no. 2." Words matter, and they so easily can be misconstrued. "What is that in the road ahead?" has a meaning somewhat different from "What is that in the road, a head?" Once, a woman who was sensitive about her weight gain got a memo from another department at her office: "You're going to owe me big girl." As she read the memo she was furious. After thinking about it she printed the memo and showed it to the woman who had sent it, asking: "If you could put a comma in here anywhere, where would it go?" And the new sentence read: "You're going to owe me big, girl." A single comma had all to do with the results of that particular communication.

In 1997 Kentucky Fried Chicken entered the Chinese market with its motto, "Finger-Lickin' Good," which was translated in Chinese as "Lick your fingers off." That was unfortunate. When Pepsi Cola entered Korea, its catchphrase, "Come Alive with the New Generation," became, in Korean, "We will raise the dead." That didn't go over so well, either. Nor did Chevrolet fare well in South America when it tried to market its Nova there. In Spanish, *no va* means "It doesn't go." Communication between cultures and languages can be tricky, indeed, and it requires great care as well at the office and at home. Using language carefully becomes very important to our overall success.

Chapter 9

"IT" HAPPENS! SO WE WORRY AND DON'T FORGIVE

*"The single biggest problem in communication
is the illusion that it has taken place."*

—George Bernard Shaw

We should never anticipate trouble, said Benjamin Franklin, who lived in quite troubled times. "Keep in the sunlight," he advised, "and do not worry about what may never happen."

"Worry is the misuse of the imagination," says author Dan Zadra. The actor Michael J. Fox said he doesn't worry because if what he fears actually does come true, he will have worried about it twice.

Columnist Harvey Mackay tells of a survey revealing that 40 percent of our worries never come to pass. Thirty percent of our worries involve past events that we can't let go; 12 percent are other people's problems; and 10 percent are imagined health issues. That leaves only 8 percent of our worries that are actually worth our attention.

Unnecessary worry blocks our leadership, as does our lack of a sense of forgiveness when we perceive that we have been wrong. Goldsmith talks about forgiveness as "the letting go of the search for a better past." In fact, in India, one of the ways that they have captured monkeys in the past is to simply put jars full of berries and roots in the woods. In the middle of the night the monkeys come down the trees, put their paw in the jar, and grab the berries and the nuts. As they try to pull their paw out of the narrow neck of the jar, it gets stuck, and in many cases they will sit there all night holding on to what they think is really important. They sometimes even fall asleep while holding on. The ranchers collect them in the morning, and there is no struggle because the monkeys have held on to the very end. And thus begins their life of captivity in a zoo.

Forgiveness is letting go of those things that aren't that important in our lives. Otherwise, we too could find ourselves led into our own kind of captivity, and we'd miss the opportunity to focus on what really matters, what we truly stand for, and how we might inspire others.

Unnecessary worry and the inability to forgive others are what often hold us back from the success that we should be enjoying. We lose the ability to effectively influence others, and as we shall see in this chapter, that has profound implications for all of us, whether we are politicians conducting world affairs or businesspeople serving customers through our personal branding, our "it" factor.

Good leaders inspire people to follow them with confidence. Great leaders inspire people to have confidence in themselves. The body of a leader is made up of three bones: the funny bone to set the tone; the wish bone to set the plan; and the backbone to stand for something or fall for anything. A Robert Frost poem contains the line, "The best way out is always through."

It's not about getting results in every aspect of our communications—trust, influence, or even our leadership—but, rather, it has to do with the journey and the differences that we make to people as we go forward. If we are to make things happen, we must strive to understand and influence others along the way as we work together toward our goals.

Stanford associate professor of psychology Fred Luskin, PhD, reported that when subjects of an experiment were asked to think about forgiving someone, the pleasure centers in their brain were highlighted during an MRI test. When his subjects remembered something from years earlier that angered them, hormones and toxins were released as if they were having that same experience all over again. This physical condition can lead to heart disease and stroke. In a real way, bitterness kills.

A LESSON FROM THE SINAI

Over the years, I've learned the people with the greatest influence are those who keep open the greatest number of options when working through any discussion. Reacting emotionally in conversations, at home and at work, can be counterproductive. The more intellectual, creative, and valuable options need time to come together.

We've all heard ourselves and others say, "Look, this is the only way to do this!" or, "This must be done this way," or, "That is not my job." We speak of requirements and expectations. A Camp David peace accord involved that kind of communication nightmare. In 1967 Israel launched the Six-Day War in retaliation for what that nation considered a violation of its airspace. Israel's action sent shock waves around the globe, and particularly in the Middle East, where Syria suffered great losses and stopped fighting in a single day. The Egyptians continued to fight for five more days until they were beaten back. It was the start of 11 years of skirmishes and bombings between Israel and Egypt, killing thousands of people.

In 1978 President Jimmy Carter brought Menachem Began and Anwar Sadat to Camp David to resolve these hostilities, which were impacting world commerce and international relationships. The Sinai Peninsula, a plot of land between Israel and Egypt, seemed to be at constant war. President Carter privately expressed his belief to both men that this land was worthless. It had no oil, and no measurably valuable farming or housing. Why all this unrest?

He finally got Began to say that he did not want Egyptian tanks parked along his border. He was overly concerned and afraid for national security. He wanted to demonstrate national defense. Well, this was news to Jimmy Carter. Nobody had ever fully understood this huge war over worthless land. President Carter pursued Egypt's desire to own the Sinai Peninsula. Why? Anwar Sadat finally said that it was a matter of national pride. He was not going to be the first leader of Egypt since the pharaohs to not have control of the

Sinai. President Carter went to work to solve their concerns and bring peace.

To this day, the Egyptian flag flies over the Sinai Peninsula. It is a demilitarized zone, patrolled by the UN to ensure there are no weapons on the Israeli border. That solution took 11 years and thousands of lives to accomplish, and required critically clear communications and candor. Candor isn't as easy as we think. We sure like our egos!

There is a clear lesson here for the corporate world. We need to be more creative, questioning, concerned, and resourceful as we deal with the many issues we face each day. We need to focus on our relationships and our mutual needs and motivations so that all parties in any discussion can get what they need when they need it.

PERSON OVER PROCESS

In 2003 Warren Buffett and his company Berkshire Hathaway met with the executives of Wal-Mart to discuss a major billion dollar deal. Buffett was interested in purchasing McLane Distribution, which distributes groceries and nonfood items to convenience stores, drug stores, theaters, and others. At the time, McLane had sales of about $23 billion, yet operated on paper-thin margins—about 1% pre-tax.

This deal would swell Berkshire's sales figures far more than their income. It was an attractive deal. McLane was a good business (and still is), but it wasn't in Wal-Mart's mainstream future.

Now if a multi-billion dollar deal doesn't already interest you, here's where it gets downright juicy; after meeting for a mere 2 hours, both parties agreed and shook hands. The deal was done. Within 29 days the money was sent with absolutely zero due diligence being performed on Berkshire's part. (Excerpted from Tim Simpson, *Speed of Trust*)

Too often, we replace trust with process. The process reinforces our perception of rightness even as we hang over a cliff.

Jim Mazzo, the former Chairman and CEO of Advanced Medical Optics, tells of an offer that his firm made to a large pharmaceutical organization to buy technology to expand his ocular surgery business. He would pay the asking price in what should have been an easy, valuable deal for everyone involved. Then began the process with bankers and lawyers, and endless streams of communication, haggling, and debate. After many months, the deal was finally done—and the seller had lost millions as the marketplace changed and the value of the product declined.

"It would have been great for all of us if we had been able to complete this agreement sooner," Jim told the pharmaceutical company's CEO, who replied, "We have a process."

PERSONAL BRAND: THE "IT" FACTOR

The ability to inspire and influence others is highly critical in our relationships with customers and clients. It's important to remember that, to the customer, you are the company. That means your personal brand is critical not only for your success but for the company's too.

We've all been there. Someone walks into a room at a business event and suddenly the air becomes electric. Heads turn. The world pays attention, serious attention. People gravitate to that person as if to a magnet, and they engage that person in conversation, hanging on his/her every word. You have just witnessed a "Wow!" moment in real time.

Such people possess the "it" factor. It is the essence of their personal brand. It's not hard-wired into you; it's not a part of your business face or DNA; it's easy to recognize yet hard to define. Some people just have it, and we all recognize it when they do. We strive to get it, and sometimes we lose it, but even if it is lost, we can regain it. You can't really manufacture, reproduce, or create it. "It" is not a thought, purpose, plan, or process. "It" happens!

When you have that "it" factor, you see opportunities where others see obstacles. That's why we all need to embrace "it," nurture "it," give "it," and share "it."

Turns out you're not born with this quality. It is the gift of presence, and it is a gift that you can give to yourself. It's no mystery, just a blend of attributes and skills that, in the proper combination, transmits all the right signals.

YOUR PERSONAL BRAND BUILDS TRUST

Done right, the "it" factor builds trust, which leads to word-of-mouth buzz that opens up opportunities for professional and financial success. These days, with so many companies downsizing and trying to trim costs by promoting from within, trust and marketability are our two most powerful commodities.

Personal branding provides a boost to our ascent to the job we want, creating greater alignment and passion for serious work and engaging our colleagues and workforce. It renews our membership in the marketability club. It communicates who we are.

Our brand is the impression that people have of us. In business, it's important to build your brand with everyone: colleagues, bosses, direct reports, clients, and suppliers. It's impossible to go out and develop a personal relationship with everyone. Having a personal brand establishes you in a network that can provide a huge advantage.

THE ELEMENTS OF PERSONAL BRANDING

What is involved in personal branding? Branding specialist Roz Usheroff has outlined several key factors:

Communication skills: The most important aspect of "executive presence" is the ability to communicate substance. We need to share our expertise in a powerful way. To do this we need to develop communication skills in our speaking, presenting, and writing. Those who cannot convey business and technical skills won't be appreciated or recognized to the fullest.

In forensic medicine, fingerprints are highly significant, and likewise, leaders need to leave their "touch" for a lasting impression. We need to touch emotions in the people we lead and in our customers. In short, executive presence should be quiet and effortless. It should not shout for attention and interrupt.

Style: They don't use "substance" and "style" in the same sentence for nothing. As much as we might like to think style doesn't matter, the way we dress and how we conduct ourselves speak volumes about us as professionals.

Physical presence: Physical presence is more than your clothing; it's your spirit and energy, your body language. We need to move through the world with a purpose, reflected in how we walk, sit, and stand. Are we confident and approachable? Your body language sends subliminal messages about your state of mind.

Networking: Your network matters immensely, as part of your strategy for success and pursuing opportunities. You need to be the PR person for yourself.

Vocal skills: Many people know us only by the sound of our voices. Using your voice effectively reflects your confidence, intelligence, and passion. You need to speak clearly with animated inflections.

Manners: Poor business etiquette can wreck your career. It's simple: be gracious and treat others as you would like them to treat you. This is important whether in a conference room, a customer's office, or in the dining room.

Listening: Listeners stand out. They show themselves to be accessible and caring and interested in the speaker and what the speaker is talking about, and they encourage others to speak.

Workspace: What does your workspace tell others about who you are? Is it messy and cluttered? Maybe your life is too, and maybe that's how a prospect will imagine a relationship with you will be like. Piles of paper communicate procrastination. Getting rid of the trash will improve your image and how you feel about yourself.

Chapter 10

PRAISE, PERSPECTIVE, PRIORITIES, AND PEOPLE

"Our leadership is only on loan to us, from those we lead."

—Ken Blanchard

T he late Andy Griffith may be one of the most widely recognized of actors. He was in the business more than 40 years, and today's generation knows him too, mostly through reruns of *The Andy Griffith* Show of the 1960s. As the sheriff of Mayberry, his down-home style won the hearts of television viewers. To this day, as I flip through the channels, I find myself stopping when I see a rerun, and pausing to watch Andy's style of leadership as sheriff and parent.

In one memorable episode, his son Opie is raising three little birds in a cage. When they are big enough to fly, Andy patiently encourages Opie to let his prized birdlings go by asking him how he feels about letting them go and explaining that these baby birds need a bigger arena than a cage, a much bigger one: the sky. As Opie comes to that conclusion himself, he encourages each bird to fly and feels like a proud parent on graduation day. Afterward, Opie holds up the cage and says "Boy, the cage sure looks empty." Andy replies, "Yes, Son, and don't the trees seem nice and full?"

It's a beautiful metaphor for giving back. It's about giving to something bigger than ourselves. We can learn to look less at the empty cage and more at the beautiful world if we help others do the right things.

And it illustrates one of the fundamental focuses that leaders need if they are to influence people. They must lead through praise, offering new perspectives as they help to establish priorities, remembering, always, the importance of people, and the primacy of others.

A PERSPECTIVE ON DEDICATION

Two years ago, on a trip to Mumbai, India, I had a chance to help sales leaders improve their teamwork and communication skills. As I left, I mentioned that the information I provided could be presented on computers via a thumb drive.

"We don't have computers," a sales representative told me, nor, he said, did the managers. I suggested that the program be put on CDs to be played in their cars. He explained that they used mostly scooters and motorbikes.

He then told me about the day of an Indian sales rep: 9 a.m. to 11 p.m., and sometimes till after midnight if the physicians were performing late surgeries. The reps made 15 or more sales calls per day, reviewing perhaps eight products with a physician. (In the United States, reps make 6 to 8 calls per day.) Indian reps make calls six days a week for $6,000 a year—and they love their jobs. They are, as a whole, generous, benevolent, smart, and determined to take care of their customers and their company. It's a true ownership mentality.

And we all know people who are miserable as they get up to go to work in conditions of relative opulence. Ah, perspective.

SIX FACTORS OF SUCCESS

Let's take a look at the nature of success in business and the factors that go along with it and are important to finding it. A 2009 Gallup poll found six factors shared in common by 100 companies identified as among the best places to work in America. The six factors were: fun, fair, friends, freedom, pride, and praise.

Tom Sullivan, a noted keynote speaker, has said that PRIDE can be an acronym for "personal responsibility in individual, daily effort." Pride has a lot to do with your success at home and at work.

Tom, who has been blind from birth, has embarked on an amazing journey over the past eight years that has never been done before. His goal is to assist eye doctors with their care of patients. How can a blind man inspire, excite, and educate a doctor about patient care when he has never had the gift of sight. Never seen a sunset, or seen his wife or child's face? In 1950, Tom's doctor wanted to institutionalize him. Tom was not institutionalized, thanks to his parents and other forces which helped him attend Perkins School for the blind in Boston, where he learned to read Braille and to play the piano and sing. He attended Harvard, paying for his education by playing the piano and singing. And when he connected with Betty White, he gained fame through TV shows and concerts, including singing the national anthem at the bicentennial Super Bowl. As a youth, he learned to wrestle and was inducted into the National Wrestling Hall of Fame. He also learned golfing, downhill skiing, and marathon running, and he wrote 14 books. Are you kidding me? Progress and pride comes from setting goals and overcoming obstacles. And Tom overachieves because of an enormous fear of not being loved. As a child, the dark, scary world of blindness must have been overwhelming. His fear was so great it propelled him to heights of achievement, leadership, pride, and love that few of us are lucky to touch.

Tom shares his unique perspectives on patient care with eye doctors, who often see blindness as a failure. How often do we like our failures paraded in front of us? Tom tells doctors stories about low-vision patients who were seen by doctors after office hours because the doctors did not want patients with extremely bad eye problems in their waiting room—might be bad for business! Tom reconnects eye doctors to their role as caregivers. He emphasizes their need to know more about Braille learning centers, and to do more to help parents of children who are nearly blind. The rich learning and positive attitude Tom brings to everyone and receives from everyone he meets makes patient care better. A lot better!

ABOVE ALL, PRAISE

We say praise is important, and in many companies it's the only means by which a good performer is recognized—with a simple "Thank you." There's more to it than that. In fact, a formula for helping leaders give better praise exists. It doesn't take much more time than just saying, "Thank you," and it has tons more value: you praise employees by saying, "I really appreciate your (blank)." You fill in the blank with the appropriate value. Is the word "courage"? Is the word "pride"? Is the word "enthusiasm"? You pick the value that you think is important to those you're praising. Then you go on to specify the action they took that was so outstanding. It is important to add at the end of your praise statement the fact that their action has helped everyone see and understand how to achieve the organizational goal. In summary, to praise someone is to recognize a key value first, then the specific action they took, and how that ties back to a larger group goal.

That, in a real sense, is how you praise people, and more importantly, it is how you go on to motivate people. If you want positive movement, use praise. That's why a sense of appreciation ranks as one of the top six characteristics of really successful work places.

I have learned that praise is a medicine, and it is one not so easily administered in a world where so many people are determined to prove that they are right and the other guy is wrong. Real praise isn't just words designed to sound agreeable and supportive. Real praise reflects, rather, a genuine sense of caring about another person, and it often shows recognition of what that person has been enduring. It arises from a true perspective on the troubles we all encounter. Praise is enriching. When you feel appreciated, you are motivated to meet another day with passion.

REACHING GREAT HEIGHTS

Good leaders help others to feel in control by demonstrating that they have the situation under control. The manner in which leaders react instills confidence in others.

"True leaders are less concerned about the rewards of being a leader and more aware of the responsibility that the role brings— the responsibility for serving as a role model to those around them," authors Angie Morgan and Courtney Lynch write in *Leading from the Front: No-Excuse Leadership Tactics for Women*. And a good role model insists on preparation. That's how we learn to find true perspectives and establish priorities. When we do so, we can reach great heights.

Once, when my sons and I were visiting a simulation lab for fighter pilots, I saw a sign that pointed out that in challenging times we must rise to the occasion, and we can "only rise to our level of training." Neil Armstrong, who made that "giant leap for mankind," emphasized, after his return to Earth, that nothing could have been accomplished without intensive practice. Getting things right, he said, cannot happen without guidance, rehearsal, and practice.

Capt. Chesley Sullenberger could tell you about the importance of preparation. He was the pilot in "the miracle on the Hudson" in January 2009, when he successfully landed U.S. Airways Flight 1549 in the river, saving 155 lives after the plane struck a flock of Canada geese. Sullenberger had been involved in the first crew resource management training course, which teaches teamwork and collaboration in high pressure situations, and it was certainly a high pressure situation that he found himself in that day. He was a former glider pilot, and relied on that experience to provide a near-perfect glider-type landing in the water. His 19,000 hours of flight time over 40 years began with his award as the Outstanding Cadet in Airmanship at the Air Force Academy. He was a man used to being first. On the aircraft in the Hudson, however, he stayed to the last, making sure everyone was out.

PERSPECTIVES ON SUCCESS

I am the same age as the CEO and one of the salespeople at my company. What differentiates us besides our W-2 statements, overall responsibilities, and the fact that the others are smarter than me?

It's perspective. Our CEO has a global, business-development, and long-range strategic perspective. Our sales representative has a stronger customer focus and larger perspective on product promotion. All these qualities are important to success.

Which perspective is most important? It depends on the task, and the audience. The customer would believe the sales rep's perspective is the most important, and Wall Street would probably go with the CEO's viewpoint. The CEO would tell you that he could not do his job unless the others did theirs. So who is more important?

It doesn't matter!

That sense of importance often motivates us the wrong way. We are all anxious to be more important, or more right, or more successful than somebody else. We climb the corporate ladder so we can see our kingdom.

I've known people who climbed that corporate ladder, reaching for all the decorations of success, only to realize the ladder was on the wrong house. In your search for material success, if you sacrifice what is really important to you, you are not the winner. Instead, you lose.

The real struggle among the most successful leaders is how to have their employees be perceived as the winners. The CEO's job is to find a way to recognize and appreciate all the employees who do their jobs.

In 2007 I had the chance to interview one of the top sales performers in our pharmaceutical company. She was among the highest performing sales reps in the company's history. She had a 20-year sales career, marked by eight top-five finishes and 10 top-ten finishes. She was a perennial all-star. Although her teammates wanted to learn from her, she did not give up her secrets as she pursued a fierce work ethic. Then through her life changes and discovery, she had this to say:

> I have learned winning is more about achieving your values through work, than having someone think you're successful. We've been taught over the years that we only achieve what can be measured. If it's not measured, then it's not a result. That has driven compensation models for years.

> Yet every company has some mission statement devoting itself to high integrity or to being trusted or highly professional. How do you measure that? In essence that is why you work at a company, because of the way it makes you feel, the quality of the people or products or the customers. And yet those factors are hard to measure. If we're all playing fair—that isn't good enough. We need to be meeting our values.

Henry Ford in 1929 was losing sales, and Chevrolet came out with a straight six-cylinder engine. Ford had an idea for a v-8. He drew it up and told his engineers to further design and build the v-8 engine. They spent their time deciding who would go tell the "old man" that it couldn't be done. "I don't care," Ford said, "and don't come back to me until it's done and done right." It took a year and a half and saved Ford and changed the auto industry.

A WINNING ATTITUDE

A reporter once asked Sparky Anderson, the baseball manager of Cincinnati Reds and Detroit Tigers fame, about the pressure on him for the Tigers to win a World Series game.

"Pressure? Oh this isn't pressure," he said. It was the fans who felt the real pressure, he said. They worked hard all day, with money and time so scarce at times, yet still managed to bring their families to the stadium. "That's pressure," he said. "I'm just playing a game!"

Several years ago I heard an interview in which the famous sports announcer Bob Costas told of the greatest example of leadership in sports that he had witnessed. He told the story of John Steven Akhwari of Tanzania, who came in last in the 1968 Olympics marathon. At the closing ceremonies, he ran into the stadium, wincing in pain. Why had he kept running when it was hopeless? "My country did not send me to Mexico City to start the race," he explained. "They sent me to finish the race."

That's what it means to truly win. That's the heart of competition. It's also the way successful businesses endure and thrive. It's not about the recognition. It's about building quality and value for future generations because it's the right thing, the fair thing, the great thing to do.

THE DIFFERENCES WE MAKE

Significance is measured in the difference you make for everyone and anyone. As we saw with one of our top salespeople, the definition of success is very personal. It's about the personal triumphs and setbacks that define our character. That's it. No fancy titles, or income statements. It's who you are to you. Those with a wealth of experience who have felt a range of emotions may be better able to define themselves because they have better relationships with others.

Jim Collins, author of *Good to Great* and *Built to Last*, was recently interviewed by Jo Burkingham for *Inc.* magazine. In the interview, Collins pointed out our need to accept that we have a finite amount of time to handle an infinite amount of work. What we need to control, he said, is our time. Most of us still hear Mom's voice telling us we need to get our work done before we can play. In truth, we need to balance those needs and allot the appropriate time to each. Priorities are indeed essential.

In our pursuit of the factors of success, we must always remember that kindness is not weakness. There's a big difference. Many managers seem to believe if you aren't cranky, they aren't managing you effectively, or you aren't focused enough on your work, because work is a serious business.

Recently I was standing in a hotel lobby at a work table that was positioned outside a meeting room. My boss happened to walk past just as one of my coworkers made this comment about me: "Jim is always so nice." My boss declared to us all: "Yeah, and that's because I don't stress him enough!"

The implication was that being nice was a weakness. My coworkers fell silent, and I wasn't sure how to respond. Business is not for the faint of heart, but kindness rules. Kindness helps people to build teams, set goals, admit mistakes, adjust quickly, and grease the wheels of change. Please, don't underestimate the power of kindness or you risk alienation. Without kindness, you seriously limit your people power.

How do we measure leadership? It's not results, promotion, head count, money, or rewards. Those are the measures of *achievement*, you being proud of *you*. Leadership comes through asking how others will be doing years after you are gone. You lead by engaging their abilities and ideas.

What matters is *others*, and it's true in sales as well, particularly in this age of social media. Selling on social media is like face-to-face sales: you wouldn't walk up to someone at a cocktail party and say, "Hi, I'm Jim. Would you like to buy a watch?" Instead, you should say, "Hi, I'm Jim, and I see how things are for you, and here's an idea that I hope brings you great success." Social media is about building a connection; it is not a sales channel. Leaders build people, which is what builds business.

LEADERSHIP
BY CARING

There's a great story about Captain Michael Abrashoff who took over command of the USS *Benfold* at age 28. He had never commanded a ship before, and at the time it was the worst-performing ship in the U.S. Navy. He watched the captain of the USS *Benfold* leave the ship to an embarrassing round of boos, and cheers for his departure—in front of his family.

Michael Abrashoff was a young captain, unsure of the best way to navigate forward, so he interviewed each crew member, got to know them all, and learned about ways the ship could be more effective in the navy.

"Sir, we're just all monkeys in a tree," one seaman told him.

"Please tell me more, what do you mean?" Captain Abrashoff asked him.

"Well, sir, you're on the bridge, and when you hand out commands, you look out over a whole sea of smiling faces, like monkeys in a tree looking up to you to see what they should do next. But I'm down here in the engine room in that same tree, and I look up, and I see something altogether different."

It's not the smiling faces he sees, but the other ends.

Capt. Abrashoff realized that we're all just people, and we're all in it together. We're all monkeys in the tree doing the best that we can. And through that process he began to learn new ways to navigate the USS *Benfold*, the worst-performing ship in the Pacific Fleet.

During one of Captain Abrashoff's interviews, a crew member said, "Well, sir, we don't spend much time doing target practice because we're so busy painting the boat. See, these naval ships are made of iron. They rust, and that doesn't look very good, so we spend a lot of time painting the boat." And so, against naval policy, Captain Abrashoff went to Home Depot in San Diego and bought 10,000 stainless-steel bolts and rebolted the ship so the crew could stop painting and spend more time at target practice and doing what was necessary for the ship to be the best in the Pacific Fleet.

Within two years, the USS *Benfold* won the Spokane Trophy as the best-performing ship in the Pacific Fleet. The credit goes to the crew, and it goes to Captain Abrashoff for insisting that it was all about others. Captain Abrashoff did his two years of service, and on his last day he went to the microphone and spoke to his crew, not for 45 minutes, as the other commanders did, but for only 45 seconds.

He said, in so many words, "You know me, and I know you, and we've been in this together, and thank you."

There wasn't a dry eye on the ship.

How do we leave our jobs, the story of Captain Abrashoff asks us: to cheers, or to tears? How will we be remembered? You won't win by outworking your competition. You will win by outcaring them.

THE LEADER'S EMBRACE

In all that we do, as we dream and strive for success, we've learned that we can't run alone. We need to understand that it's about the music and the lyrics, the behaviors and the attitudes, the intentions and the actions, the mind and the spirit. It's about the employees and the community, friends and family, body and the heart. We're all angels with only one wing and we learn to fly while embracing one another.

Alex Haley, author of *Roots*, had a picture in his office of a turtle on top of a fence post. When asked by a journalist why it was there, he explained: "Every time I start reading my press clippings or believing I am really good at some piece of writing, I look up at that picture and remind myself that he didn't get there by himself."

He had help. We all need help, and to ask for, appreciate, and give back help says more about us than any of our other abilities.

None of us are all that good, but with the support of others we cannot be stopped. In the end, we win. In friendships and partnerships, in hope and joy, lies the greater victory. Trips and bonuses are nice too, and they fade. Real relationships are built through effort and shared commitment.

We all want to reach our island, the island of happiness, success, wealth, and peace. Getting there requires us to put our boat in the water and trim the sail. We need to get moving. Jim "Jimmy V" Valvano, the basketball coach and broadcaster who died in 1993 of cancer and whose foundation has raised multimillions for cancer research, said that nothing ever happened without enthusiasm. You need a sail and wind to get to that island, and we complain so often that there's no wind, or too much. We cannot control that. We can only control our sails.

Only when we can accept our internal conditions and embrace our creativity and energy to make decisions and drive outcomes can we forget about the external conditions that we can't control. Sunny days or rainy days, we still must move our boat forward, with our sails fully under our control. And if we find those sails to be tattered and worn, perhaps that just shows how much we have learned about ourselves.

Our moods are a natural ebb and flow of emotions. Our attitude is a choice. In fact, if you just act happy, the muscles and facial expressions used to project that positive attitude will convince your brain you are happy and not just acting as if you were.

I struggle sometimes with that issue of authenticity. Leaders are asked to be authentic. At the same time, we hear remarks such as, "Well, act your way through it. Act in front of a customer as if you care. Act as if you're enthusiastic, even when you feel bad." And I've had people in business say to me, "How am I supposed to act when I don't feel that way? I'm not really being authentic." It hurts us even more because authenticity, for many of us, is a core value.

I asked my good friend, Pastor John Steward, about that, and he said, "Jim, there's a lot of times on Sunday morning that I get up in front of congregations, and I'm talking about love, hope, and joy, and I don't feel it. I've had challenges at home or problems of my own, and yet I find myself determined and dedicated to something larger than my own selfishness."

When we come to see that authenticity is about reaching for something higher than ourselves, we become less selfish. We tune in to others. We become less sensitive to our own issues. Rather, we are authentic in dealing with the needs of our customers, our companies, our research departments, our families, our friends, and our community. In the end we are true to our own values. That's the core of leadership.

ALL IN ALL, A
GOOD DAY

C indy and I were friends at work before Teri passed. She asked about Teri and the kids and seemed kind, as were so many people at work.

After Teri's death, we talked about the challenges of raising kids, and those talks at times ended in laughs. She was raising two hellions—I mean, wonderful kids—of her own.

One day, as we talked in the hall, she asked if I'd ever seen Ms. Saigon, and if I would like to join her that Saturday.

"You mean, like, a date?" I asked.

"Sure," she said. "Why not?"

It wasn't long before my kids were enjoying her cooking. My cooking had been improving, and I was surprised to learn some things, including the pitfalls of preparing bacon in a toaster oven. And who knew you should add milk to Kraft mac-and-cheese?

After a year and a half of dating, I asked Cindy to marry me— three times! She said yes each time. I asked her during a getaway weekend in Arizona. When we came home, she gave me back the ring and left me alone for a few minutes with her kids, Robbie and Kelly. I asked them what they'd think if I were to ask their mom to marry me. They squealed and ran to get their cameras. Cindy came downstairs, and I popped the question, and we all laughed and cried. Then she returned the ring and later, at my house, I asked my own children how they'd feel. More squealing and running for cameras— and "yes" one more time.

All in all, a good day.

There would indeed be challenging days to come after we married. With five teenagers at home and their summer vacation approaching, Cindy eventually decided to leave her full-time job— "retire," as she put it—so that she could be there "to keep the kids from drinking beer for breakfast."

Jeff, our oldest child, continued his struggles in school. He was the only child to call Cindy by her name; the others called her Mom. He could be funny, and he was smart, though he needed to apply himself. I felt that through all his struggles, I needed to keep the lines of communication open. We always got along, even in strife.

One day in his senior year in high school, I pressed him to get his English essay completed. He assured me he would. A few weeks later, he received a letter in the mail from Saddleback Community

College announcing he had won an award in the Orange County short story contest for his school essay. I was so happy for him and asked how he had done in that English class. He got a D-minus. For this award-winning story, he said, the teacher gave him an F because he had forgotten the due date and had handed it in a week late.

On the day of the award ceremony, as I drove with Jeff to the college, we saw his name on the college billboard for top writers. And in a room of 100 teachers, students, family, and local media, we waited for his moment of recognition, which came with a $100 prize and a plaque.

The announcements began with the third-place winner, a young woman who claimed her award for her story "My Mother the Flower."

Jeff turned to me. "Are they going to read the titles?"

"It looks that way. Why?"

"Oh, this may not be good," he said.

"And now, the award for second place," the announcer said. "Jeff Trunick, for his story 'Kill the Head and the Body Will Die!'"

And so my tattooed son lumbered up to the stage, in his black shirt, black pants, black boots, and earplugs. The audience applauded tentatively, they were more curious than congratulatory.

I smiled and turned to the aghast, elderly English teacher next to me. "That's my boy!" I told her. Jeff and I laughed all the way home.

We all need laughter, and often it surfaces just when we need it, to lighten those moments that might prove difficult. I think of a time when Jeff and I were watching TV in the family room a few months after Teri's death. It was one of those too-few occasions when he wasn't out with friends. "Dad, give me the channel changer," he ordered abruptly. Like a good parent who wants his child to be polite, I said: "Jeff, what do we say? I bet you could find another way to ask for it." His response: "Okay, give me the channel changer, damn it!"

Sometimes leadership means letting things go. We all need to laugh, whether at home with our families or at work with our colleagues. Laughter is the lubricant of life. It keeps things flowing and moving, and it gives us perspective so that we don't blow out of proportion some word or perceived misdeed. When you can laugh at yourself, you win those around you.

After Teri died, Jeff, like our other children, felt troubled. At the age of 15 he had fallen into alcohol and drugs and gone into a tailspin with his studies, communication, and family support. He was gone a lot, riding around with friends.

Meanwhile, I was trying a pull my life together and deal with our new blended family. Jeff was getting high and drinking. He barely attended classes and drifted away. His attitude seemed to be: Who cares? Mom's gone. Dad's remarried. Why not do whatever I want? My heart was crying out, "Oh, Jeff, why are we going through this? I need you more than ever."

Jeff went to "parties" with his best friend, James. One night, when Jeff was 19, he gave his car keys to another friend, Jack, so Jack could drive James home. As Jack was driving, with James sleeping in the back seat, he lost control of the car and it flipped. James flew out the back window and died on the side of the road.

Jeff awakened me the next morning, as I was in Boston on business, to tell me James had died. After that, Jeff went further downhill. Telling me he was straightening himself out, he borrowed money from me, and I realized I was being a codependent to his problem and enabling him to be alone with his demons. He moved into an apartment with his girlfriend, and they began a steady diet of crystal meth. At age 20, he was a six-foot-one-inch skeleton, weighing 108 pounds. His eyes were dark; his mind was mush. I realized our problem had gone beyond terrifying. I only had three choices: I could watch him go to jail; I could watch him die; or I could try to get him to a hospital. The only action I could control was getting him to the hospital.

We met interventionist Jeff VanVonderen, and began a process in which we wrote letters about our shame over his behavior and our desire for him to seek help. At 20 years old, my son was of age, so I couldn't force him into rehab. I had to sell him on the idea, with the support of the family, to make that happen.

After I called him most of the night—at his apartment where he faced eviction—to propose meeting me, he finally answered the phone at 8 a.m. Totally trashed the evening before, he just hadn't wanted to answer the phone. I went to his apartment and brought him to my house, not for breakfast but to talk. As he sat confused and disoriented, I saw his moment of decision. It was when James's mother, Pat, read her note of sadness and pain that Jeff decided to go to Pac-Hills, a rehab center in Laguna Beach. Pat has not since kept in touch. I think that she reached her limit of sadness and pain and moved on, leaving southern California.

I saw so clearly how a steady diet of praise means everything to success. After six months in rehab, Jeff did remarkably well and started to go to his support meetings in Orange County, where he regularly got buttons marking his monthly anniversaries of drug-free living. He got the chance to help out at meetings.

After a few more months, he told me he was going to move to New York to follow a girlfriend. Against my wishes, he packed up his materials and left for New York at age 21. Jeff was gone.

I called him there regularly. On one call, I asked whether he had started to go back to his support meetings. He said he hadn't, and as I struggled with my feelings, I tearfully told him how important those meetings were for bettering his life.

"Dad," he said, "when I was going to the meetings in California, they told me I was getting better. I got buttons to encourage me. They applauded me, and I had people praising me, telling me how proud they were of me. But when I went to the meetings here, I found myself being scolded, told I was no good, suggesting that if I didn't do what they told me I was going to die, and that I was a disappointment to everybody."

I learned then that praise means everything in the most real sense of life. It is essential to the core of leadership.

When Megan lost her mom to leukemia, she felt devastated. She felt loss and anger all at the same time, and that led to serious misjudgment about her own sense of self.

She began cutting herself. I wanted answers. For instance, since she was cutting herself in obvious places on her body, wasn't it clear

ALL IN ALL, A GOOD DAY

that she wanted her issues to be noticed and confronted? We had some tough conversations, and, eventually, went through counseling.

What I have learned is that it is the search for answers about others' behaviors that leads directly to the heart of our own leadership. Leadership seems to me to be more about exploration and discovery than it is about mapping and planning. Leadership is always measured in the eyes and soul of the other person. Great results are only valued in terms of the long hours, creative thinking, and personal sacrifice that it takes to achieve them. The greatness of the result matters little compared to the learning gained in the process. I learned that for all my determination and effort to serve as a great mom and great dad I was falling short on both—as measured by results. As measured against my heart, learning, and love, I am a great dad.

Still, Megan continued cutting herself. At age 16 she was hanging out with people I didn't know, and I thought were unclean. She quit cross-country running, and became argumentative for almost no reason.

Cindy and I returned home one Saturday to find Megan at the bottom of the stairs with a hefty bag full of clothes, announcing, "I'm leaving." We went to the kitchen, dismissing her comment before deciding we should talk to her about it at once. By then she had walked out the front door and climbed into a car with her girlfriend, who was also 16. Megan was gone.

We didn't know what to think. Was our daughter gay? We shrugged and thought she'd be back for school on Monday. Six weeks went by without a word. Her brother Brian told us which apartment complex she was living in, with three others who were several years older.

Cindy and I decided we only had one option: to send her to a rehabilitation center. Why had she run away? We were an affluent, caring, nurturing, God-centered, and loving family. She'd had great grades and extracurricular success. And now this. This was indeed a challenge, and it seemed Cindy and I too were learners.

We decided to have Megan forcibly removed from the apartment. We were determined to "save" her. Through months of counseling and therapy we kept asking ourselves, "When is she going to change, grow up, learn, and realize the error of her ways?"

The day we had her forcibly moved, custodial caregivers and an out-of-state van pulled up near the apartment. Cindy asked her son Robbie to try to coax Megan from the apartment. Megan wouldn't talk to Cindy or me, and Robbie was the only sibling we thought she might listen to. Robbie approached her apartment and talked her into coming outside, where two custodians wrapped her up and locked her into the van to drive away. Cindy was waiting 200 feet away and handed Megan some clothes as the van stopped to roll the window down. Megan was furious and screaming and vulgar, and she didn't know she was going to a different state.

She was sent to Utah and placed in a lock-down environment where the dorm rooms had bars and guarded doors a country club jail for wayward youth, as it were. She spent a year there. We had weekly phone calls and quarterly, face-to-face, visiting (5 hours from our home) and counseling sessions, at which Megan repeatedly told Cindy and me that we just didn't get it!

Megan came face to face with so many adopted, fostered, and undirected children that she began to learn. She completed her high-school requirements—two years of high school—in one year. She graduated from the counseling program the same day. Her grades turned out to be remarkable, as was the support of the counselors.

Only after intense soul searching and introspection did I realize that her rehabilitation in a far-away boarding school was not about her changing—she is still professed gay. It was more about our changing. Cindy had been thrown into this world and was only trying to help; Megan needed to change; and we all grew. I should have been more involved and more supportive earlier in Megan's attempts to deal with death. I had my own challenges, and Megan, as the only woman in the house, wanted to feel more needed.

I thought all this great therapy was going to help her "see the light" and grow up. Rather, I learned that I was the one who needed the counseling. I needed to let go of my desire to see her become the straight-As student, the fastest girl on the track team, and the daughter who went to the prom with the nice boy next door. Even as I tried to define my role as both a mom and a dad, it was still about me.

I was seeing truly and fully the role of others in all our lives. Cindy led me when I was trying to nurture. Cindy saw the problem more clearly and acutely. Her perspective was invaluable in the face of death and destruction. I wanted to minimize everything. I just didn't see the true picture.

We cannot do it alone. We are built to lead and be led—all of us. So much depends on values and timing. John Maxwell asks a great question about winning without self-interest. When we believe that winning is about crossing the finish line first, or climbing the mountain to the very top, we find ourselves lonely there. Today's real leadership is about going back down the mountain, embracing all those who helped you along the way, and taking them all back up to the top of the mountain. There, when you have reached that height, you stand in the back for a group picture. Have you noticed that on any awards program, the winner invariably does what amounts to that very thing? It's because real winners know that they cannot do anything by themselves. And so they offer their thanks.

Ken Blanchard tells the story of what happened at the Special Olympics in Seattle several years ago. As several young runners took off on the 100-yard dash as fast as they could, one boy fell and yelled out in pain. All the runners stopped and looked. One by one they returned to their fallen competitor. They picked him up, and they all ran together across the finish line. It was a six-way tie for first place. Winning is about doing the right thing. Only together does it matter.

I learned that leadership is truly about letting go of the desire to improve the outcome of others; it's about supporting, loving, and listening to others' desires to improve their own outcomes. That fundamental shift changed my relationship with Megan, as I expressed these thoughts in a letter. I wrote many letters and had weekly counseling with Megan, and I recall trying to express myself as someone who wanted to love her for who she was—warts, bumps, pains and all—not for whom I wanted her to be.

I learned that I am a wonderful parent after all and I have normal, wonderful kids who aren't me. And since then, I have held tightly to our love and strived to let go of trying to define Megan. She will define herself and design her own legacy.

My saga of parenting continues. Jeff, at age 29, is independent and finding his way. Megan is doing the same.

Brian is lost. I put him for a third time into a structured living environment, after psychiatric testing and further psychological counseling. I saw him for a few hours on Christmas Day in 2012, and now that he has left that home, I have no idea where he is.

I once talked to Brian about those notes in his lunch box that his friend gave him long ago at school. He doesn't remember them. Clearly they held a much more powerful meaning for me than for him. I'm glad he had that friend. He always seemed to be in need of more friendships.

In high school he had some friends who turned out to be abusive to him. He hung out with them when I was enjoying my new marriage and wanted time alone with my new wife on Friday nights. He was the only child still at home, and so he visited with those dismissive and verbally abusive friends. It is hard to forgive them or myself, and now, at the age of 26, Brian seems lost to me, and alone. His phone is turned off, and I've had no word from him in a long time.

Our quest to get to the core of leadership is supposed to be hard. Other animals on our planet are in a food chain. They are bait. We humans make decisions, choices, and we can reason. Yet despite our advancements, our brains sometimes seem very primitive. We ask for help, and sometimes it's not there, and it's not supposed to be there.

I think of a caterpillar morphing into a butterfly. As a butterfly emerges from the chrysalis, it endures an arduous process of cracking wings and breaking casings that appears extremely painful. But if we cut the casings to help the butterfly attain its freedom, the wings will not gain the strength to fly. The butterfly will die. The strength to live, and to fly, is born of the excruciating pain.

Obstacles can be our inspiration. A blind person conquers a mountain. An amputee runs in a marathon. Ever tell your children that they cannot do something? They can't wait to do it.

Let us all learn through life. Bring on the challenges that will take us to the core of leadership.

THE CORE OF
COACHING

A COACH'S CORNER

Hey JT,

I have an employee who has had great success, and in our growing video business we have asked her to train another new hire. She begrudgingly does it, and tells us how this new person isn't getting it, and is a waste of her time. What should we do?

A: Well, you had one problem: train the new hire. Now you have two problems. Whoops—that wasn't the plan! Yeah, these are common. Your trainer—does she see the benefit to being a trainer? Is she motivated to learn how to improve this skill? If not, I'd go another direction, and direct your top performer, who you want to be a trainer, to those skills where they are the most motivated and valuable. Then train the new hire with all the expectations, knowledge and skill to be great in the next 60 days. Don't train the new person on future skills if they don't have the foundation clear and observably accurate!

Hey JT,

I've got a top performing manager and he is doing great. His team values him greatly—and yet he is almost invisible at our advertising and billboard creation meetings, conference calls, and other task force and home office interface opportunities. How do I get this guy out of his shell?

A: Does he want to come out of his shell? The issue is two-fold. 1. Is this an expectation of his job? If so, you should assess him against that competency of managing up or increasing his organizational savvy. One of his goals maybe to align his people's efforts with organizational goals, and if his interactions minimize that alignment, he needs to be aware and improve. 2. If the problem is minimizing his advancement/promotability—which he doesn't seem to want, and his results continue above expectations—let it ride! To each their own, in terms of visibility. Forcing it won't work. He has to want for something more

---

Hey JT,

My best account manager interviewed for my job, and I got it. We had been friends over the past few years, even shared award trips together, and now I hear rumors he is saying bad

things about me to others. He seems distant, and I was told he was upset he hadn't gotten the promotion. What now?

A: Well, good luck with that—next question? Kidding. This is unfortunate and needs leadership-less management, meaning, telling him you're in charge, and here's how it's going to go—not good. First, gain all the perspective from interviewers as to why he did not win the promotion. Break this down for yourself as areas of strength and opportunity for growth. You should utilize the learning your management gained from his interviews as guidelines for his development plan to further achieve his career goals. Second, let him share or even vent; encourage the real ugly story by listening as peer, not boss. Determine with him ways you can act, behave and actually collaborate for both your benefit and goals. Don't ignore rumors, just don't act on them.

Hey JT,

I am getting pressure from our president to drive better results. My effort is nearly 80 hours a week and I have all my accounts doing all they can do—the economy is working against me and customers, and my management just won't hear it. The situation seems impossible.

A: It may be impossible—and not for you to decide the larger outcome. The opportunity here is to look inside what you can control—and it's not the economy or your company's expectations. When you say "all accounts doing all they...," I would look deep inside these comments. Really—"all"? In some regard, this may stifle your chance to come up with unique and creative approaches, as it allows you to throw up hands in frustration, as opposed to trying novel ideas to work around the problem.

"The best way around a problem is through it!"—Helen Keller

Hey JT,

I have had great results over the past few years, and now I am not making quota, which is frustrating, since others in our electrical products organization are growing sales faster than myself. Should I work with a business coach to re-establish myself on top?

A: Maybe. Before getting a coach, make sure you are fully self-analyzing your current situation. The hardest person to sell is a friend. Have your long time customers become more friends? Are you more the visitor and less the seller? What are other top performers doing? Investigate. Maybe more training will help, as you identify areas necessary to grow. I am a fan of networking and collaboration, which will really help before external coaching.

P.S. Coaches help you for the current role and mentors should be picked to assist your learning for the next role.

Hey JT,

I am having great results, although I have only been with my current firm 1 year. My 10 years of sales experience with a competitive grocery goods company in the same industry has prepared me well. However, I feel micromanaged on all kinds of administration, from my calendar, to the targeting of leads and routing to get more sales calls per day. Did I mention that I am doing great in my results? How can I gain more independence? I'd like to tell my bosses, "Leave me alone; I'll produce!"

A: Oh, I hear the great results piece—I also hear your "1 year" too. Pretty sure of yourself... and maybe with good reason. A question, though: are you being micromanaged, or resisting a new cultural norm by bringing your 10 years of experience with you as a badge of achievement, or are you just not willing to learn a new culture? They may sense you comparing them to your "old place." Quantity and quality work go hand in hand, and quantity shouldn't be minimized, just because it feels less intellectual or creative, than quality. Your comments suggest you are measuring results in 1 year, and maybe more acceptance of quantity goals and planning may minimize the micro-management. Try asking, "If I improve administration and routing, can we talk less about it?"

Hey JT,

I have worked my butt off for this huge account. Every time I get close to an agreement, I find myself chasing more details and compromises to do staff training, copies of reports, other commitments from side-parties. All out aggravating: all my hard work, and still no sale.

A: Tough one! New rule: hard work doesn't lead to sales. We grew up believing, "Early bird gets the worm," and, "Success doesn't happen without hard work," and, "99 percent perspiration and 1 percent inspiration," all of which feed our high value of work ethic. Customers tease us with requests-we-think-lead-to-sales tactics because it works. It delays their decision and they get the best of all competitors vying for the business, with you doing extra work. Set expectations with your customers: "For all my effort—what behavior will change for you?" With that expectation-setting step, and agreement to outcomes, you don't waste your time. We've conditioned our accounts to believe all our hard work is free, in the name of relationship—neither of which leads to the sale.

"If you don't ask—you don't get."—All successful people

Hey JT,

I am losing business to a competitor who is telling my customers, "I need an order from you now, or I'll lose my job." My customers always agree to support my competitor, to some extent. What can I do?

A: OK. Fix this or I'll fire you! Well, that's not right. It's the guilt trip, begging, leverage and pity strings all pulled at once. It is very short-term, manipulative, unsustainable, undifferentiated, and unethical tactic. I had a friend in a patio-enclosure business that was faced with the same scenario with his customer, and he tried saying, "Would you try pleading and begging with your customers to gain their business—like you'll go out of business without their buying a patio enclosure?" And if you did that to your customers, how would you feel? Kinda slimy? Those qualities shouldn't be rewarded. You might try saying, "I appreciate you sharing with me how we can serve you best, and let's focus on those benefits to make this product decision. Good for us!" Quality should rule, in our products and people dealings.

Hey JT,

I have a number of customers telling me how much they value and like me, and they use my office furniture samples and other materials—and yet my results in this account are stalled. No changed behavior. When do I lower the boom?

A: Lower the boom—is that like bombing them? Not good. When they ask for things (and they should do the asking, without you volunteering all your goodness), ask them how using your samples or materials will be used. And now you are discussing product benefits, and not giving everything away.

Hey JT,

I recently have hired 3 new associates. Only 1 has worked out and even he is performing slightly below expectations. I was sure they would all work out. Where am I most likely missing?

A: It may be in these 3 key thoughts:

1. Have you done a thorough job, going through multiple interviews, with various others commenting on the candidate, and observed them actually doing the job, if even for a day? You'll learn more from your and their feedback on the actual job, instead of just doing well in an interview.

2. Have you checked their past performances, attitudes and motivations, toward certain activities? Have you gained enough reference and evidence of past experiences supporting their work responsibilities, tied to behaviors you expect?

3. Has work process, team and new hire expectations, been set for everyone?

Hiring team members starts with them joining. The work begins, then, to understand how to get better results than when you were functioning without them.

90 percent of your work is done if you get the right person. 90 percent of your work is in front of you, if you get the wrong person for that job!

Hey JT,

Exhausted, dude! I mean, there is no time to get all this done. Can you get me a 25th hour each day? Thanks; that would be huge!

A: Sure, and what would you do with that 25th hour? You say family, friends or workout—but you'd mostly do more e-mails! Unless, like a professional athlete, you can commit your time to your deepest values! Then you'll minimize those non-priorities you spend so much time on, because they are fun or easy, and by crossing them off your list, you can feel accomplished. But not happy and not sure what to say no to? Know that we get lost in "can't get it done."

"Don't mistake activity for achievement."

"Better to have a life plan over a business plan!"

Hey JT,

I can't manage everything. Some stuff with people… Shouldn't we just let go? My #1 rep., in fact, a national 2-time top performer, is regularly late on expense accounts, misses conference calls, and other admin. because they are out selling! I mean, you'd let that go, right? They are driving the results.

A: Nope. That's their area for learning and growth. They are driving results for themselves and the organization, but hurting your leadership and team's commitment to organizational goals. Team results will overshadow any one territory's results. Manage it—with your top performers held to the same standard as all performers. Your people already see it, and they may be looking for ways to undermine you—you could be encouraging it more than you know.

Condoning incompetence for any team member, particularly the teacher's pet, is erosion of high standards, and the beginning of the end. Accountability rules for all! Culture eats strategy for breakfast!

Hey JT,

My accounts are great partners. Last year, I won a trip to France for my efforts at our software company. This year I was close to making it, and falling a little short—I opened up to my best accounts, that I needed a favor to win this year's trip and asked if they could order more. They did and I am enjoying wine at a French bistro. Once in while you need a favor?

A: Cool, but how do you feel, really? Top of the world? Beg your way to success? We have an obligation to treat customers as kings! Treating our customers as tickets to our gifts, though… How's that feel again? It's the reverse of "buy or I'll lose my job," and it's still manipulative. I did a research project, years ago, and in a private screening off-camera, a large account told me about a rep. winning a trip to Hawaii if he ordered more parts in his service center. He said, "That's like me asking you to buy my car, so I can win a trip." I asked him, "What kind of relationship do you think they thought they had with you, to even ask such a question?" He said, "Oh, I knew him for years—great guy—loved him. But as we grew, we started seeing other groups, and we don't do business with that guy now."

———

Hey JT,

Sometimes I will make the sales call. I lead managers in a handbag company, and in the really important accounts, I find greater results if I jump and make the sale. It's a problem, because sales are good, and I'm stretched too thin. I know my salespeople need to sell, but it's just so clear to me what needs to be done—and we git 'er done!

A: Well, you git 'er done. And actually you hire people to do their job, and if you do their job and yours, well… You may be super-salesperson, and your people learn to count on you, more than they learn how to be successful when you aren't around. And their success when you are not there should be your goal. Your goal needs to be more sustainability and less execution. "Teach a man to fish…" You know the rest.

———

Hey JT,

I am under so much competition in my high-end upholstery business, and competition is fierce. I'm getting sales and results are good, but loyalty seems to be shrinking among my top accounts?

A: Well, you'd better get working! Wrong. Better get them working! Put your loyalists and advocates to work. It's just like in school, when your favorite teacher most likely made you stretch or added a level of accountability and extra work to your plate, which led you to becoming a leader in the classroom. I got a science degree because of the prodding, pestering and challenging of my high school biology teacher (thanks, Paul Ruley of Cincinnati Anderson High School!).

Have your top accounts become loyalists, because they publicly speak on your behalf, and lead the charge for you.

___

Hey JT,

I coach this guy over and over, and truly nothing improves. What am I missing?

A: Well, you can lead a horse to water, and you cannot make it do backstrokes. He has to want to do backstrokes! If he can do backstrokes, why doesn't he?

Good luck... You've got lots of listening and investigation to finalize. He's motivated to do something; you just need to tie his motivations into your goals!

___

Hey JT,

My best manager just got an offer from our direct competitor, promising more money and career growth. I can't afford to lose her, and she just up and told me she's leaving for this great opportunity. Now what?

A: See ya! Don't accept her resignation. It may not do much good, except to buy time to help her think through her real options for her career: what she is running to or from? Be sure that she isn't making an emotional decision. Why does she want to leave? Why do you want to keep her? We too often take our people for granted, and correct their errors, calling that feedback. New jobs sound great, until 2 years from now, when she'll feel the same way about her new job. Is she really looking at all angles? It may be too late, or it may be a chance to learn from each other to find ways to change for the better. Surprises are no fun, from leadership down or leadership up.

Over-communicate or look in the mirror for how you want the rest of your reports and teams to interact.

I am 2 for 4, in "not accepting" resignations. Two I wanted to keep, and I'm glad I did. Two were leaving without my counsel, and we all survived and grew regardless!

Hey JT,

I am leading with total conviction, our products and people. I am sharing organizational goals with my team, and they love their jobs and me, and yet we are on the bottom of results. Argh! What am I missing?

A: A clear definition of what "good" looks like. It requires winning. Not being #1 on all projects, or having the best sales results, or meeting all project deadlines ahead of schedule or under budget, or rallying speeches without clear behaviors. I think we spend too much time talking about the results we expect to achieve, and not nearly enough time on what behaviors are going to change to achieve these high expectations. And perfection is less valued than progress. We all love a winner, but we love an underdog even more. An underdog is more like us, and we feel good when they overcome odds and win. Not perfection; just progress. Once they win, we pull for the next underdog!

Set goals you can make progress. Report those victories and celebrate small wins. Bigger wins will come, if you praise the small wins, and set the course for future behaviors of winning.

———————————

Hey JT,

I am getting pressure to encourage my team members to look at promotions into another high growth division inside our multi-national company. We've built a high-performing team and they don't want to leave, and getting them promoted seems to work against their goals. So do I meet the needs of my company over my team? And my results may suffer while I fill their vacant territory. Team player—I dunno?

A: Well, you do have a higher responsibility to fuel the corporate organizational value, beyond your manager bonus? And I don't believe your management wants to see you promote people when they don't want promotion. How good are you at encouraging their growth beyond where they are today? They may not want it, but do you give them full balance of perspective, given your stated concern for your bonus? Have you had lateral or promotional assignments to broaden your perspective? And you should be pleased the organization values your leadership; they want to populate their future success with your team. Very exciting!

Hey JT,

It's me, Dave. Remember I told you about Steve—the older gentleman, who came into the grocery store where I was working as a clerk, and he was looking for special grape flavored ice bars. One night, while shopping at Target, I saw the grape bars, and I bought bunches! The next day, when Steve showed up, I said, "I think we have grape bars." And gave Steve exactly what he wanted. Steve was blown away.

A few weeks later, Steve called me, and asked if he was still interested in following through on my interest in a career in audio/visual production. I was stunned and said sure. Steve offered me a new job, which was exactly what I was hoping to achieve. After a few weeks I asked Steve why he had hired me, with no experience. Steve smiled, and said, "You know the grape bars you got for me, when it was not of any financial value for you, and you weren't specifically looking for recognition or appreciation? What I need in my small company are good people who care, and can be trusted above all else. That's you, and I'm glad to have you learning on my team." How do I repay Steve, for giving me this gift of a career I love?

A: Say thank you, with a note to his wife or close friend, of how much you respect and appreciate Steve. Then pay it forward to someone else. You win. That's living leadership.

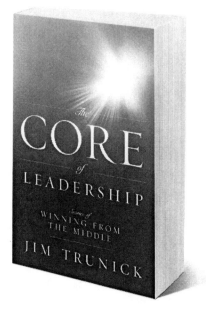

How can you use this book?

MOTIVATE

EDUCATE

THANK

INSPIRE

PROMOTE

CONNECT

Why have a custom version of *The Core of Leadership?*

■ Build personal bonds with customers, prospects, employees, donors, and key constituencies

■ Develop a long-lasting reminder of your event, milestone, or celebration

■ Provide a keepsake that inspires change in behavior and change in lives

■ Deliver the ultimate "thank you" gift that remains on coffee tables and bookshelves

■ Generate the "wow" factor

Books are thoughtful gifts that provide a genuine sentiment that other promotional items cannot express. They promote employee discussions and interaction, reinforce an event's meaning or location, and they make a lasting impression. Use your book to say "Thank You" and show people that you care.

The Core of Leadership is available in bulk quantities and in customized versions at special discounts for corporate, institutional, and educational purposes. To learn more please contact our Special Sales team at:

1.866.775.1696 • sales@advantageww.com • www.AdvantageSpecialSales.com

CPSIA information can be obtained at www.ICGtesting.com
Printed in the USA
LVOW07s1540010913

350448LV00005B/13/P